DECORATING THE KITCHEN

87 Projects & Ideas to Update the Kitchen

The Home Decorating Institute®

Copyright © 1994 Cy DeCosse Incorporated 5900 Green Oak Drive Minnetonka, Minnesota 55343
1-800-328-3895 All rights reserved Printed in U.S.A.

Library of Congress Cataloging-in-Publication Data Decorating the kitchen / the Home Decorating Institute. p. cm. — (Arts &
crafts for home decorating) Includes index. ISBN 0-86573-363-5 ISBN 0-86573-364-3 (pbk.)   1. Kitchens. 2. Interior decoration.
I. Home Decorating Institute (Minnetonka, Minn.) II. Cy DeCosse Incorporated. III. Series.   TX653.D397 1994 643'.3—dc20
93-41246

CONTENTS

Kitchen Decorating

Cabinets, Countertops & Floors

Painting & Wallcovering

Window Treatments

Accessories

KITCHEN DECORATING

*The kitchen is often
the hub of activity
in the home.*

Although the primary function of the kitchen is food preparation, it is commonly a gathering spot for family and friends, especially if it includes an informal eating area.

With so much time spent in the kitchen, one can easily become tired of the decorating scheme. But, for fear of high remodeling costs, it is often unchanged for many years. Surprisingly, there are many changes that can be made to the decorating scheme of a kitchen without either the expense or the inconvenience of remodeling.

Consider giving the cabinets a face-lift by painting them with glossy white enamel for a traditional kitchen, or with a farmhouse finish that has country charm. Then add new hardware to complete the look. You can also change the color of kitchen appliances without replacing them.

Create useful accessories, and sew window treatments that complement the style of decorating you like. For a traditional look, make shelves of white lattice and sew awning valances in bold green and white stripes. Add character to a country scheme with crocheted rag rugs, handmade peg rails with crackled finishes, and ruffled stool covers. Or decorate a transitional or a contemporary kitchen with checked walls, simple U-shelves, or hand-painted placemats.

All information in this book has been tested; however, because skill levels and conditions vary, the publisher disclaims any liability for unsatisfactory results. Follow the manufacturers' instructions for tools and materials used to complete these projects. The publisher is not responsible for any injury or damage caused by the improper use of tools, materials, or information in this publication.

TRADITIONAL KITCHEN

*Traditional style
offers a timeless look
that is rich and refined.*

The cabinetwork sets the tone of a traditional kitchen. With many styles to choose from, the cabinets may be quite plain or have elaborate moldings and panels. For two distinctly different looks, choose from the bright, cheerful finish of white enamel or the rich warmth of natural wood. The final touch is the hardware of brass, black iron, porcelain, or crystal.

Accessories in a traditional kitchen add to the look of refinement and richness. Enliven the kitchen with an abundance of lush ivy or flowers. Fill a traditional iron pot rack with polished copper pans, and hang a ceiling fixture of brass and glass.

Make a dramatic statement by choosing striking colors for room surfaces and fabric. Fabrics, often in polished cottons, may be patterned in florals, plaids, paisleys, or stripes.

Several items shown here can be made following the instructions in this book:

*1. Enamel paint finish
(page 40).
2. Awning valances
(page 67).
3. Tablecloth (page 78).
4. Cross-stitched linen
(page 84).*

*5. Ruffled stool cover
(page 95).
6. Upholstered chair seat
(page 99).
7. Lattice shelf (page 119).
8. Collection (page 124).*

MORE IDEAS FOR A TRADITIONAL KITCHEN

Traditional iron pot rack *is filled with polished copper pots.*

Silk cabbages *add cheerfulness to the traditional kitchen. They may be used as a table centerpiece or on shelves and windowsills.*

Natural wood cabinets, *traditional in style, are topped with a decorative railing (page 27) that provides the perfect framework for a group of colorful pottery items.*

White enamel cabinets *(page 40) are accented with black iron handles. The black-and-white striped awning (page 67) and varied black accessories complete the look.*

COUNTRY KITCHEN

Filled with American tradition,
a country kitchen holds
cherished memories of the past.

With its home-style atmosphere, the country kitchen has lots of sentimental appeal. Farm-style tables, peg rails, and other practical furnishings predominate, offering simple variety. Cluttered displays of cooking utensils are kept handily within easy reach.

Light woods combine with dark. Farmhouse and crackled paint finishes are frequently used, giving an aged look. The serviceable fabrics used for window treatments, table linens, and other accessories are often plain cottons or a haphazard mix of colors and patterns.

Displayed collections may include antiques and rustic boxes. For textural interest, honeysuckle vines and dried herbs may be hung from a peg rail at the window. For a touch of color, herbal oils and vinegars rest on the sill.

Several items shown here can be made following the instructions in this book:

1. Farmhouse finish (page 46).
2. Painted check design (page 49).
3. Cafe curtains (page 62).
4. Crocheted rag rugs and mats (page 89).

5. Herbal wall hanging (page 102).
6. Flower box (page 104).
7. Peg rails (page 109).
8. Collection (page 124).

MORE IDEAS FOR A COUNTRY KITCHEN

French country look *has white enamel cabinets (page 40) as the backdrop. The cheerful setting is created by adding blue and yellow patterned fabrics, fruit-embossed earthenware, and a baker's rack.*

Natural wood cabinets *feature porcelain knobs for a country emphasis. Advertising art, an egg basket, and other country pieces are set off by contrasting bright blue tiles.*

Painted detailing *brightens the country-style chair at left. The chair seat is upholstered as on pages 99 to 101.*

Asymmetrical window treatment has one cafe curtain panel (page 64) and a single shutter.

Wheat sheaf (right) is bundled and tied to the back of a farmhouse chair for country charm.

Southwestern influence inspired this casual country kitchen. The bordered placemats are sewn as on pages 78 to 81.

TRANSITIONAL KITCHEN

*An eclectic mix of decorating styles
gives the kitchen a look that
is exciting and personal.*

I n transitional decorating, contrasting styles are used in a single room, appealing to the individual tastes of family members. A range of furnishings sit side-by-side in an interesting mix of old and new, shiny and dull, textured and smooth.

Dissimilar elements are often integrated, with cabinets serving as a unifying backdrop. Terra cotta pots can rest on a contemporary shelf painted in black enamel. Or utensils of unfinished wood may stand in a shiny pot.

Fabrics can set off or complement the other furnishings. Choose fabrics in bold, abstract, or ethnic prints. Or for a clean, straightforward look, opt for simple fabrics like cotton muslin.

Several items shown here can be made following the instructions in this book:

1. Wineglass rack (page 27).
2. Color-washed finish (page 44).
3. Butterfly swags (page 70).

4. Placemat (page 78).
5. U-shelves (page 114).
6. Lattice shelf (page 119).
7. Collection (page 124).

MORE IDEAS FOR A
TRANSITIONAL KITCHEN

Peg rail, with its country influence, is used as a curtain rod for this easy swagged window treatment. The homespun fabric, fringed at the ends, drapes softly.

Copper, terra-cotta, and raffia repeat the warmth of natural wood cabinets. The accessories are country in style, but their shiny new surfaces are quite contemporary.

U-shelves (page 114) are stacked on the countertop for easy-to-reach storage.

Painted stool coordinates with the printed fabric of the placemat (page 78). The stool makes convenient seating at the countertop.

Jars tied with raffia are filled with various pastas for textural interest.

Cabinets,
Countertops
& Floors

MODIFYING CABINETS

Cabinets are a primary consideration in kitchen decorating. Because of their size, they become a backdrop for kitchen furnishings and accessories. Several things can be done to change cabinets without replacing them. Fresh paint, new knobs and drawer pulls, or additional trims and moldings can significantly change the look of cabinets with only a small investment of time and money.

By keeping the cabinets rather neutral in style, you can easily change the look of the kitchen from country to traditional to modern with the change of kitchen accessories. Or emphasize a particular decorating style by making a strong statement with the cabinets, perhaps crackling them for the country look of aged paint.

Stained wood finish *(left).*

Color-washed finish *(right and on page 44) and moldings (page 22).*

Crackled finish *(below left and on page 42).*

Painted finish *(below right and on page 40) and moldings (page 22).*

Farmhouse finish (above and on page 46).

Painted check design (below and on page 49).

Enamel paint finish (above and on page 40).

Color-washed finish (below and on page 44) and moldings (page 22).

CABINET MOLDINGS

Give cabinets a new look by adding mitered moldings to the existing cabinet doors. A number of decorative trims are available at woodworker's stores, from rope moldings to dentil moldings. Stain or paint the trims in a contrasting or matching color.

Use the molding as a frame or border on a flat-panel door. Or position the trims around a raised or recessed door panel, for added definition. For more emphasis, a pair of moldings can be used as a double border. Plan the placement of the moldings on the door panel; if the molding is not being positioned along the edge of a raised or recessed panel, mark the placement for the outer edge, using a pencil.

Remove the cabinet doors before you apply the moldings. For easy installation, the moldings are cut, using a miter box and a backsaw with a fine-tooth blade, then applied to the doors with wood glue. Use the glue sparingly for a neat application; wood glue holds securely even when only a small amount is used. Secure the moldings with clamps until the glue has dried, protecting the moldings with a scrap of lumber under the clamps.

If the moldings are being applied to beveled or routed edges, it will be necessary to adjust the angle of the cuts somewhat by sanding the ends of the mitered molding strips. It may be necessary to fill small gaps between the strips with wood filler or putty.

Because there will probably be slight differences in the measurements from one door panel to another, measure the panels on each side before cutting the moldings, to ensure an accurate fit.

HOW TO APPLY CABINET MOLDINGS

MATERIALS

- Decorative moldings.
- Miter box and backsaw with fine-tooth blade.
- Wood glue.

- Clamps.
- 220-grit sandpaper.
- Stain or paint as desired.

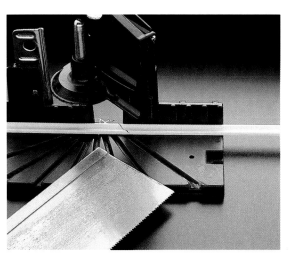

1 Measure and mark length of one molding strip on outer edge; mark angle of cut. Using a miter box and backsaw, cut a molding strip at both ends. Repeat to cut the remaining molding strips.

2 Check the fit of the molding strips; sand the corners, using 220-grit sandpaper, as necessary for proper fit.

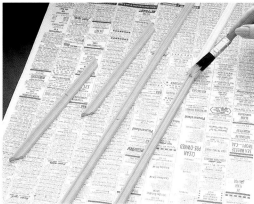

3 Paint or stain moldings if contrasting trim is desired; allow to dry.

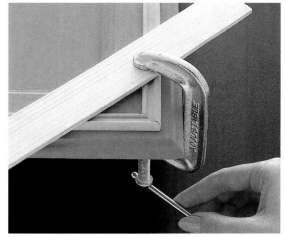

4 Apply wood glue sparingly to the underside of the molding. Position on door, and clamp it in place. To protect the trim from the clamps, use scrap of lumber. If there is any excess glue, remove it immediately, using scrap of wool fabric.

5 Remove the clamps when the glue has dried thoroughly. Fill any gaps between the molding strips at the corners, using wood filler if trim is painted; touch up paint. If trim is stained, fill gaps with putty that matches the stain.

CABINET
HARDWARE

Old cabinets are sometimes revitalized by simply changing the hardware. With new hardware, basic cabinets can be transformed from traditional to country or contemporary. In addition to the numerous hardware styles, you can select from materials including metal, crystal, porcelain, wood, and plastic. Most hardware stores carry a wide selection, but, for even more variety, shop a specialty store or mail-order supplier of decorative hardware. Or for unique pieces, visit secondhand and antique stores.

Because the simplest procedure for mounting new knobs or pulls is to use the existing holes in the cabinet, you may want to use your current hardware as the starting point for size. However, by filling the old hole or holes and drilling new ones, you can change the location of the hardware, or change to a knob or pull that requires a different spacing for the holes. Before you drill any new holes in the cabinet, try patching one of the existing holes and touching up the finish, to be sure you are satisfied that the old holes will not be noticeable. If your finish cannot be touched up satisfactorily, you can use ornamental plates, or *escutcheons*, to cover the previous holes.

To help you make a final selection, some stores allow you to purchase knobs on approval, or to apply any returns toward future purchases. Some stores will charge a modest restocking fee. Buy a single knob of the style or styles you are considering before purchasing a complete set for all the doors and drawers. Mount the knob on a cabinet door that is frequently used, and see how it looks and how it feels in use. Some attractive hardware does not operate comfortably.

HOW TO CHANGE KNOBS & DRAWER PULLS

1 Decide on placement of new knob or pull; consider using existing holes. Fill one hole that will not be used with wood filler; sand smooth, and touch up cabinet finish. If satisfied with results, fill and touch up any other unused holes.

2 Mark the placement for new holes on cabinet. Center-punch hole, using awl. Drill a new hole. Screw the new knob or drawer pull to cabinet; for glass knobs, avoid overtightening screws, which can lead to eventual breakage.

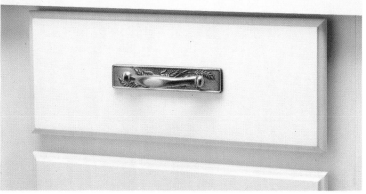

Escutcheon may be used behind a drawer pull or doorknob to conceal previous holes when the cabinet finish does not touch up satisfactorily.

CABINET DETAILS

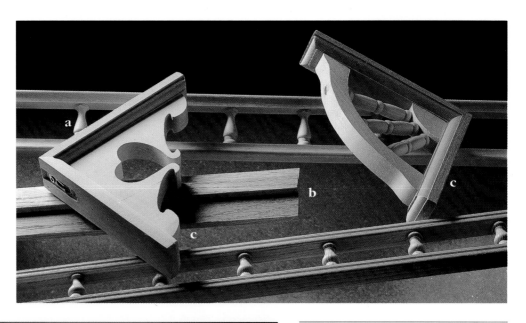

Even simple cabinets can look impressive with the addition of decorative details, such as brackets, gallery railings, or wineglass racks.

Decorative millwork, *(right) available from woodworking stores, includes gallery railings **(a)**, moldings for wineglass racks **(b)**, and decorative brackets **(c)**.*

DECORATIVE BRACKETS

For a nostalgic look, add decorative shelf brackets under the wall cabinets. For an elegant look on white painted cabinets, use brackets with gingerbread detailing, giving a look that is reminiscent of the decorative millwork of the Victorian era. Or for a country look, choose brackets that have cutout hearts or spindled brackets.

The brackets are simply nailed into the bottom of the wall cabinet, instead of attached to the wall. The brackets may be positioned in several ways, depending on the design of the cabinets and the look you prefer. On some cabinets, the brackets can be positioned flush with the outer edge of the cabinet. On others, the brackets may "stand proud," or extend slightly beyond the cabinet edge; or they may be "positioned inboard," or recessed.

Decorative bracket *(left) with a heart cutout adds to the country look of this cabinet.*

Wineglass rack *(opposite) provides a practical and decorative way to hold stemware. The rack is easily installed under the wall cabinets.*

GALLERY RAILING

Add architectural interest to cabinets with decorative spindled railings, available in many styles to suit your taste. For an elegant traditional kitchen, gallery railing adds a crowning touch to wall cabinets, but gallery railing is equally suitable for cabinets in a casual country kitchen.

Premade railing is available in lengths from 18" to 72" (46 to 183 cm); more than one length may be necessary, depending on the size of the cabinets. The spacing between the spindles varies with the style of the railing. The railing can be mitered, using a miter box and backsaw, for a neat appearance at the inside or outside corners on the cabinets. In order to cut mitered corners in the railing, plan the placement so you can avoid positioning a spindle at a corner of the cabinet.

Gallery railing *adds interest at the top of a basic cabinet.*

WINEGLASS RACK

A rack for stemware can be mounted under the wall cabinets, offering a practical and esthetic form of kitchen storage. The displayed wineglasses themselves become a decorative element. A molding designed for this purpose is available through specialty woodworking stores and by mail order. The molding is sold in predetermined lengths that can be cut to fit the space under the cabinet.

If the bottom shelf of the wall cabinets is recessed, fill in the recessed area with plywood before installing the wineglass molding. This allows you to slide the foot of a wineglass in and out of the rack easily and without breakage. Use one or more layers of plywood to equal the depth of the recess. Cut the plywood to fit in the recessed area from side to side and from back to front, and secure the plywood to the bottom

shelf with wood screws, inserting the screws from the inside of the cabinet.

Cut the wineglass molding to the same length as the distance under the wall cabinet from the wall to the front edge of the bottom shelf. The molding strips are spaced far enough apart to allow for the foot and stem of the glasses. If the center of one molding strip is placed about 4" (10 cm) from the center of the next, a wide range of glassware sizes will fit in the rack.

Install one additional strip of molding for each row of glassware; for example, install five strips of molding for four rows of glasses. For a neater appearance, cut the angled side from the end strips with a tablesaw, radial-arm saw, or jigsaw; or have them cut at a cabinet shop.

HOW TO INSTALL DECORATIVE BRACKETS

MATERIALS

- Decorative brackets.
- Paint or stain and clear acrylic finish; wood putty to match stain.

- 4d finish nails; nail set.
- Drill; 1/16" drill bit.

1 Paint brackets, or apply stain and clear acrylic finish. Determine the location of the brackets; they may be flush to the cabinet, stand proud to protrude slightly beyond cabinet, or be positioned inboard.

2 Drill two pilot holes for nails at 45° angle, drilling from outer side of bracket; drill through bracket and into, but not through, bottom of wall cabinet. Nail bracket to cabinet.

3 Repeat step 2 from inside of the bracket. Set all nails, using a nail set. Touch up nail holes with paint, or fill holes with putty to match stain.

HOW TO INSTALL A WINEGLASS RACK

MATERIALS

- Molding for wineglass rack.
- Plywood and 8-gauge flat-head wood screws, if cabinet bottom is recessed.

- 8-gauge flat-head wood screws for securing molding strips, three for each molding strip.
- Drill; 3/32" drill bit; 11/32" countersink bit.

1 Screw plywood to bottom shelf, using 3/32" drill bit if bottom is recessed. Plan and mark placement of molding strips, including the end strips.

2 Cut end strips (page 27). Mark the placement for screws on all the molding strips; predrill screw holes through molding strips, using 11/32" countersink bit.

3 Mark the placement for screws on bottom of cabinet, using molding strips as guides; predrill screw holes, using 3/32" bit. Secure the molding strips with screws.

HOW TO INSTALL GALLERY RAILING

MATERIALS

- Gallery railing.
- Paint or stain and clear acrylic finish; wood putty to match stain.

- Miter box and backsaw.
- 4d finish nails; nail set.
- Drill; 1/16" drill bit.

1 Plan placement of railing so spindles will not be positioned at corners of cabinet and so railing will be 1/8" (3 mm) from front edge; railing may stand proud to protrude beyond edge, or be positioned inboard.

2 Measure length of cabinet; add 1/8" (3 mm) for each corner to this measurement if railing will stand proud, or subtract 1/8" (3 mm) for each corner from this measurement if railing will be inboard.

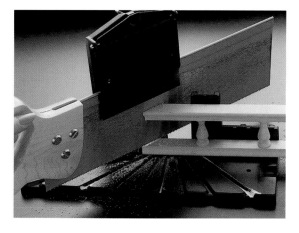

3 Determine the number of railing lengths needed for cabinet length; use angle cuts between pieces if more than one length is needed. Mark finished length of railing on the top rail. For a mitered corner, mark the angle; cut, using a miter box and a backsaw.

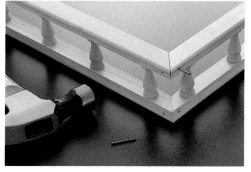

4 Glue and nail corner miters, predrilling nail holes with 1/16" drill bit. Apply stain and acrylic finish, or paint the railing.

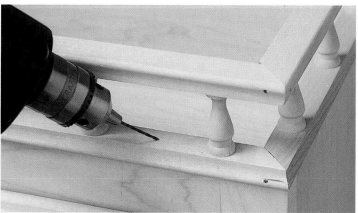

5 Reposition railing above cabinet. Predrill holes for nails at a 45° angle, spacing them at 2-ft. (0.63 m) intervals; drill through railing and into top of wall cabinet. Nail railing to cabinet.

6 Set the nails, using a nail set. Fill holes with putty to match stain, or touch up nail holes with paint.

MORE IDEAS FOR CABINETS & APPLIANCES

Lighting tube may be used under the cabinet. Use a battery-operated tube or one that can be plugged into an outlet.

L-shelf allows you to better utilize under-the-sink storage space. To support the shelf, use small brackets inserted into drilled holes on the sides of the cabinet. A pull-out wire drawer is used under the shelf for additional storage.

Knife drawer insert *is easily made by attaching blocks of wood, spaced ⅜" (1 cm) apart, to a thin plywood base; the base fits the bottom of the drawer.*

Recycling containers *(right) can be conveniently housed on a pull-out shelf attached to a cabinet door.*

Appliances in outdated colors *can be restored by replacing exterior panels, if panels are available for the model you have. Or have kitchen appliances professionally painted by a special process called electrostatic painting. This process produces a positive electrical charge in the paint and a negative charge on the appliance, to eliminate the risk of overspraying. Refer to the Yellow Pages under Painters.*

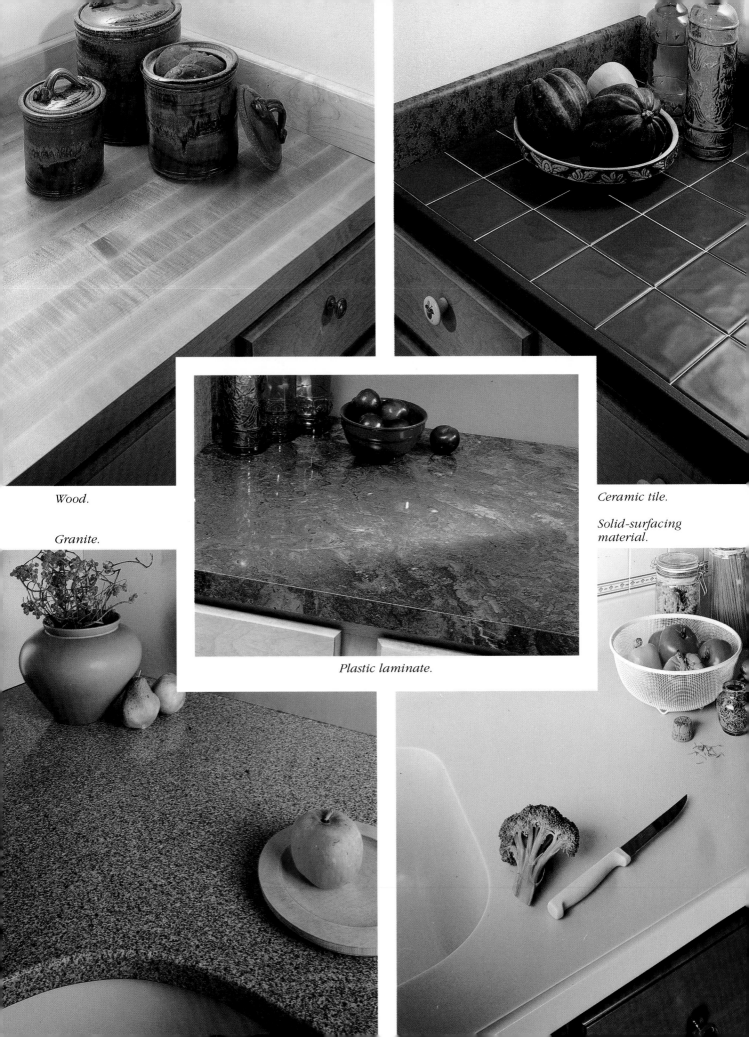

Wood.

Granite.

Plastic laminate.

Ceramic tile.

Solid-surfacing material.

SELECTING COUNTERTOPS

When a kitchen is remodeled or redecorated, the countertops are among the most frequently replaced items. Several materials are available, including plastic laminate, solid-surfacing material, wood, ceramic tile, and granite. Cleaning and maintenance are important considerations when selecting the countertop material.

Some materials are stain-resistant and are less likely to scratch or chip than others. The countertop can blend modestly with the other furnishings, or it can be quite dramatic or luxurious. Whichever approach you choose, keep in mind that countertops can last for many years, making it worth while to select them carefully.

SELECTING COUNTERTOPS

MATERIAL	DESCRIPTION	ADVANTAGES	DISADVANTAGES	MAINTENANCE
PLASTIC LAMINATE	Colored or patterned paper bonded with plastic resin, such as Formica®.	Wide range of colors and patterns; easy to clean; very low in cost.	Scratches and chips; seams are noticeable; cannot place hot pans on countertop; cannot camouflage repairs.	Clean with soap and water; remove stains with nonabrasive cleanser.
SOLID-SURFACING MATERIAL	Synthetic material such as Corian®, some resembling quarried stones; ½" to ¾" (1.3 to 2 cm) thickness.	Luxurious; custom-molded to fit cabinets; durable; scratches and burns can be sanded away.	High in cost.	Clean with nonabrasive cleanser; sand to remove scratches and burns, using 550-grit sandpaper.
WOOD	Usually maple or oak; usually 1¾" (4.5 cm) thickness.	Natural beauty; scratches and burns can be sanded away; moderate in cost.	Not waterproof; warping may occur; less durable than other countertops; can collect bacteria; can stain.	Clean with oil-based soap such as Murphy's®; sand to remove scratches and burns, using 220-grit sandpaper, followed by water sealer.
CERAMIC TILE	Glazed or porcelain; usually ¼" (6 mm) thickness. Use grout with latex or polymer additive.	Wide range of colors and designs; easy to install; easy to repair.	Grout shows soiling; grout difficult to keep clean; can crack or chip easily; moderate to high in cost.	Clean glazed tiles with soap and water; clean porcelain tiles with oil-based soap such as Murphy's; if grout with latex or polymer additive is not used, apply grout sealer every three months and regrout as necessary.
GRANITE	Natural quarried stone; usually ½" to ¾" (1.3 to 2 cm) thickness.	Luxurious; extremely durable; will not burn; does not scratch or chip easily.	Can crack; difficult to repair; limited color selection; can stain; seams are noticeable; high in cost.	Clean with warm, clear water and dry with cheesecloth; use a three-part cleaner once every two years to clean, seal, and polish.

Ceramic tile.

Carpet.

Wood with clear finish.

Vinyl tile.

Solid sheet vinyl.

SELECTING FLOORING

New flooring can significantly change the look of the kitchen. However, depending on the type you select, it might also be a significant investment. Flooring that has a prominent pattern or a trendy color can quickly look outdated as styles change. For this reason, many people prefer to select subtle designs and neutral colors. These styles can also give you more flexibility in changing the color scheme of the kitchen as your tastes change.

There are many possible materials that are suitable for kitchen floors, each with advantages and disadvantages. Consider your own life-style and the wear the flooring will be subjected to by your family. For example, it may be especially important to select a flooring that is easily cleaned if you have small children or pets, if you spend a significant amount of time cooking and baking, or if you enter the kitchen directly from the outdoors.

SELECTING FLOORING

MATERIAL	DESCRIPTION	ADVANTAGES	DISADVANTAGES	MAINTENANCE
WOOD WITH CLEAR FINISH	Strips, planks, or parquet tiles.	Natural beauty; long-lasting; timeless appeal.	Scratches; scuffs; not waterproof; magnifies room noise; moderate to high in cost.	Sweep or vacuum; wash as directed by the manufacturer; may need refinishing or recoating after years of use.
VINYL TILE	Mastic-applied or peel-and-stick.	Easy to install; easy to repair; low in cost.	Limited color and design options; seams between tiles fill with dirt; traffic areas show wear; tiles can pop up.	Sweep or vacuum; damp-mop.
SOLID SHEET VINYL	Wear coat of the flooring may be vinyl or urethane.	Practical; can be used over subflooring with slight imperfections; comfortable underfoot; low to moderate in cost, with price comparable to quality.	Depending on quality selected, may show wear in traffic areas; may stain; may tend to scuff, tear, or gouge.	Sweep or vacuum; damp-mop.
CERAMIC TILE	Glazed with a shiny or matte finish; or unglazed with the same color throughout. Use tiles with a Porcelain Enamel Institute (PEI) rating of 3 to 4+ and use grout with latex or polymer additive.	Luxurious; wide range of colors and designs; timeless appeal; suitable for high-traffic areas, especially unglazed tiles; long-lasting; good for moisture.	Chips, scratches, and cracks, especially glazed tiles; hard surface to stand on; slippery when wet; magnifies room noise; grout collects dirt; moderate to high in cost.	Sweep or vacuum; damp-mop; if grout with latex or polymer additive is not used, apply grout sealer every three months and regrout as needed.
CARPETING	Industrial grade is recommended.	Comfortable underfoot; warm; diminishes room noise; wide range of colors and patterns; disguises mildly uneven floors; moderate in cost.	Shows aging and soiling in high-traffic areas; avoid spills on carpet whenever possible; tends to stain; do not use outdoor carpeting, because it permits passage of water.	Vacuum often; spot-clean with appropriate stain removers; shampoo or steam-clean; reapply stain repellents after three cleanings, if desired.

Painting &
Wallcovering

PAINTING
WOODWORK & WALLS

There are several painting techniques that are both functional and decorative for kitchens. Because kitchens are subjected to heavy use, select a paint that gives a durable finish. Use a high-gloss latex enamel for a durable, smooth finish on cabinets and furniture. Low-luster latex enamel is also durable and may be used for cabinets, furniture, and walls. If flat latex paint is used, a clear acrylic finish may be added for more durability; however, it may yellow the paint color.

Since kitchens usually have an extensive amount of woodwork, they offer the perfect opportunity to use decorative paint finishes. For a traditional finish, try the clean, bright look of white enamel. To show off the grain of the wood, yet add a subtle tint of color, try a color-washed finish. Or for the worn, lived-in look of country, use either a crackled or farmhouse finish. For a dramatic look, try a painted check, applying the paint by stamping the design with cellulose sponges.

PREPARING THE SURFACE

To ensure good paint adhesion, it is important that the surface be properly prepared. Wash off any grease and dirt, then rinse with clear water.

Glossy surfaces, such as those that have been previously varnished or painted with enamel paint, should be sanded and then wiped with a tack cloth to remove any grit before painting.

To protect the surrounding area, use drop cloths and painter's masking tape. Painter's masking tape is recommended because it is easily removed without damaging the surface underneath.

Apply a primer to unfinished wood or wallboard. The primer helps the paint adhere to the surface without seeping into the wood or wallboard. Also apply a primer to a previously varnished surface before painting it.

Paint finishes shown opposite include: crackled finish (upper left), color-washed finish (lower right), farmhouse finish (lower left), and printed check design (background).

PREPARING SURFACES FOR PAINTING

SURFACE TO BE PAINTED	PREPARATION STEPS
UNFINISHED WOOD	1. Sand surface to smooth it. 2. Wipe with tack cloth to remove grit. 3. Apply primer; use a stain-killing primer on knotholes to seal them and prevent paint from yellowing.
PREVIOUSLY PAINTED WOOD	1. Clean surface to remove any grease and dirt. 2. Rinse with clear water; allow to dry. 3. Sand lightly to remove any loose paint chips and to degloss and smooth the surface. 4. Wipe with tack cloth to remove grit.
PREVIOUSLY VARNISHED WOOD	1. Clean surface to remove any grease and dirt. 2. Rinse with clear water; allow to dry. 3. Sand to degloss the surface. 4. Wipe with tack cloth to remove grit. 5. Apply primer.
UNFINISHED WALLBOARD	1. Dust with hand broom or vacuum with soft brush attachment. 2. Apply primer.
PREVIOUSLY PAINTED WALLBOARD	1. Clean surface to remove any grease and dirt. 2. Rinse with clear water; allow to dry.

ENAMEL PAINT FINISH

The timeless look of white painted cabinets is appropriate for any decorating style. With the use of good equipment and high-quality paint, you can achieve a professional-looking finish on most wood types. This finish is not suitable for oak because of its open grain; the color-washed finish (page 44) is recommended for oak cabinets.

The enamel paint may be applied with a high-quality paintbrush. However, for best results when painting large areas like cabinet doors and drawer fronts, it is recommended that the paint be applied with a sprayer. The use of a sprayer prevents any brush strokes or ridges caused by a paintbrush, paint roller, or sponge applicator.

There are two main types of paint sprayers: airless and air. Although airless sprayers are known to clog and apply paint unevenly, air sprayers perform with excellent results.

The air sprayers are a commercial grade of sprayer referred to as LPHV, meaning low pressure and high volume. Available from rental stores, they apply paint in an even coat without clogging and with minimal overspray. They are easy to use, even for do-it-yourselfers. The width of the spray area and the amount of the paint that is released are adjustable. Because the operation instructions may vary somewhat from one brand to another, practice on a large sheet of cardboard until you are accustomed to using the sprayer and have the spray flow properly adjusted. After each use, clean the sprayer according to the manufacturer's instructions.

Use a high-gloss latex enamel paint for a durable, smooth finish. For a smooth application, dilute the paint with a latex paint conditioner, according to the manufacturer's instructions. The ratio of paint to conditioner varies, depending on whether a sprayer or paintbrush is used. Dilute only the amount of paint that you intend to use in a day, and use the same ratio each day. Before applying the paint, prepare the wood surface as on page 39.

HOW TO APPLY AN ENAMEL PAINT FINISH

MATERIALS

- High-gloss latex enamel paint.
- Latex paint conditioner, such as Floetrol®.
- LPHV air paint sprayer, available from rental stores.
- High-quality synthetic paintbrush.
- 220-grit sandpaper.
- Tack cloth.

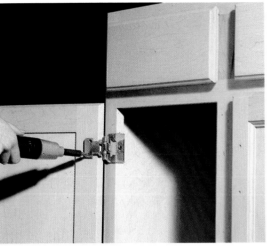

1 Unscrew the doorknobs and drawer pulls; remove cabinet doors and drawers. Prepare all wood surfaces (page 39). Mask off any surfaces that are not to be painted.

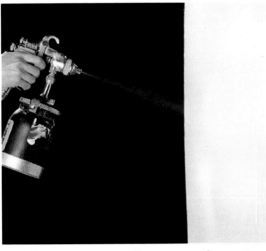

2 Fill air sprayer according to manufacturer's instructions. Practice painting on large sheet of cardboard, adjusting spray flow for a smooth, light application of paint with no runs.

3 Spray the cabinet doors and drawer fronts in a clean, well-ventilated area, applying light coat of paint. Clean the sprayer. Allow paint to dry for 8 hours.

4 Paint cabinet interiors and edges of cabinets, using paintbrush; allow to dry for 8 hours. Apply additional coats of paint as necessary.

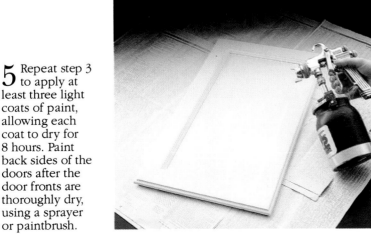

5 Repeat step 3 to apply at least three light coats of paint, allowing each coat to dry for 8 hours. Paint back sides of the doors after the door fronts are thoroughly dry, using a sprayer or paintbrush.

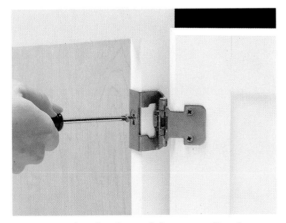

6 Secure doorknobs and drawer pulls when paint is thoroughly dry. Hang cabinet doors.

CRACKLED FINISH

This paint finish transforms wooden kitchen cabinets, furniture, and accessories into pieces with the timeworn look of antiques. Crackling, a technique developed in response to the increasing appeal of aged furnishings, uses contemporary products to imitate the effects of aging and weathering on paint.

A base color of paint is applied to a prepared wood surface, followed first by a crackle medium, then by a top coat of paint in a second color. Almost instantly, the crackle medium causes the top coat of paint to crackle randomly, revealing the base color. To give an even more aged appearance, artist's oil paints can be rubbed randomly onto the crackled surface. A clear acrylic finish is applied as a final coat for durability.

Acrylic and latex paints can be successfully crackled; be consistent in using either acrylic or latex paint for the base coat and the top coat. Because the composition of paints varies from brand to brand, some paints may not crackle as desired. Test the products on a scrap of lumber before working on the actual project, varying the length of time the crackle medium sets before the top coat of paint is applied. The thickness of the top coat can also change the look of the crackling. Because the crackle medium may tend to run, apply it horizontally whenever possible.

For a prominent crackling effect, select light and dark contrasting paint colors. For the optional artist's oil paints, select a color similar to the base coat to mix with a gray or brown. This gives a muted effect that is compatible with the color of the crackling.

Prepare the wood surface as on page 39. A crackled finish can be applied to unfinished wood or previously varnished or painted wood, provided the surface is clean and sanded; if the wood has not been previously painted, apply a coat of primer before applying the base coat of paint.

HOW TO APPLY A CRACKLED FINISH

MATERIALS

- Crackle medium, such as Quick-Crackle™.
- Paint in two colors for base coat and top coat.
- Artist's oil paints in two colors, selected as described opposite, optional.
- Clear acrylic finish.
- Paintbrush.
- 220-grit sandpaper.

1 Prepare wood surface (page 39). Apply a base coat of paint in desired color to the wood surface. Allow to dry.

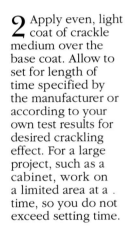

2 Apply even, light coat of crackle medium over the base coat. Allow to set for length of time specified by the manufacturer or according to your own test results for desired crackling effect. For a large project, such as a cabinet, work on a limited area at a time, so you do not exceed setting time.

3 Apply paint in a contrasting color; paint will crackle soon after it is applied. Allow top coat to dry.

4 Give crackled finish a more aged appearance, if desired, by mixing two artist's oil paints together. Rub small amounts of mixed oil paint onto the crackled surface, following wood grain; reapply until the desired effect is achieved. If too much oil paint is applied to an area, remove excess by sanding lightly with 220-grit sandpaper; wipe sanded surface with tack cloth.

5 Apply one or two coats of clear acrylic finish, for added durability.

A subtle wash of color gives an appealing finish to wooden cabinets and accessories. This finish works for all decorating styles, from contemporary to country.

For color washing, a flat latex paint is diluted with water. Applied over unfinished or stained wood, the color wash allows the natural wood tone and grain to show through. The lighter the original surface, the lighter the finished effect. To lighten a dark surface, first apply a white color wash, followed by a color wash in the desired finish color.

If you are applying a color wash to a varnished surface, remove any grease or dirt by washing the surface (page 39). It is important to roughen the varnish by sanding it, so the wood will accept the color-wash paint.

HOW TO APPLY A COLOR-WASHED FINISH

MATERIALS

- Flat latex paint.
- Matte or low-gloss clear acrylic sealer or finish.
- Paintbrush.
- 220-grit sandpaper.

1 Prepare wood surface by cleaning and sanding it (above); if surface is varnished, roughen it with sandpaper. Wipe with tack cloth.

2 Mix one part flat latex paint to four parts water. Apply to wood surface, brushing in direction of wood grain and working in an area no larger than 1 sq. yd. (0.95 sq. m) at a time. Allow to dry for 5 to 10 minutes.

3 Wipe surface with clean, lint-free cloth to partially remove paint, until desired effect is achieved. If the color is too light, repeat the process. Allow to dry. Lightly sand surface with 220-grit sandpaper to soften the look; wipe with tack cloth.

4 Apply one or two coats of clear acrylic sealer or finish, sanding lightly between coats.

FARMHOUSE FINISH

The worn painted woodwork of a country farmhouse can be duplicated by following a few easy steps. Use this finish to give cabinets an authentic country look. Or use it for an accent piece like a shelf or peg rail.

Start by mixing equal parts of denatured alcohol and clear shellac in a reclosable jar or can; then add aniline stain powder, available from specialty woodworking stores. This mixture, called *aniline-tinted shellac,* is brushed onto the wood surface, followed by latex paint.

To achieve the farmhouse finish, apply denatured alcohol after the paint is dry; then rub the surface with a lint-free cloth and, if desired, with sandpaper. This dissolves the shellac, mixing the paint with the aniline-tinted shellac. The degree to which the finish appears worn can be varied by the amount of rubbing or sanding. When using aniline-tinted shellac and denatured alcohol, work in a well-ventilated area, wearing rubber gloves and a painter's mask.

The amount of aniline-tinted shellac you will need varies considerably with the size of the project, from less than

1 c. (237 mL) for small projects to ½ gal. (1.9 L) or more for kitchen cabinets. Measure and record the amount of each ingredient used, so the exact proportions can be duplicated if the original supply is not enough to finish the entire project.

The farmhouse finish may be used for unfinished or previously varnished wood. Before you begin, sand the surface with 220-grit sandpaper and wipe it with a tack cloth to remove any grit. If the wood has been previously varnished, sand it well to thoroughly dull the surface. Do not apply a primer.

For good contrast, use a light paint color over a dark aniline-tinted shellac, or a dark paint over a light shellac. To achieve more color variation and depth when dark paint is used, you may want to apply artist's oil paints to the finished piece.

Test the technique on scrap lumber, to check the colors you are using and to determine how much rubbing or sanding is needed to give the desired effect.

HOW TO APPLY A FARMHOUSE FINISH

MATERIALS

- Latex paint.
- Denatured alcohol.
- Clear shellac.
- Aniline stain powder in walnut, cherry, or other desired wood tone.
- Artist's oil paints in two colors, optional.
- Natural-bristle paintbrush.
- Synthetic paintbrush.
- Reclosable jar or can for mixing aniline-tinted shellac.
- Rubber gloves; painter's mask.
- 100-grit and 220-grit sandpaper.
- Tack cloth.

1 Mix equal parts of denatured alcohol and clear shellac in a jar or can. Add a small amount of aniline stain powder to tint the mixture. Test the stain on scrap lumber to check color; add more aniline stain powder, a small amount at a time, until the desired intensity of color is achieved.

2 Apply one or more layers of aniline-tinted shellac, using a natural-bristle paintbrush. The more layers applied, the darker the stain. Allow to dry; aniline-tinted shellac dries quickly.

3 Apply a moderate to heavy coat of latex paint over dry aniline-tinted shellac, using synthetic paintbrush. Allow paint to dry thoroughly.

4 Wet lint-free cloth with denatured alcohol; rub onto painted surface, wearing rubber gloves and painter's mask. For a more aged look, apply denatured alcohol and rub the surface with 100-grit sandpaper; then lightly sand with 220-grit sandpaper.

5 Sand and rub the edges and prominent details more than rest of the surface, for appearance of natural wear. Wipe the surface with tack cloth. Over dark paint, apply artist's oil paints, if desired, as on page 43, step 4.

Checked wall adds visual interest to the space above the cabinets. A blend of blue, green, and gold paint gives a subtle textural effect.

Checked backsplash area is sponge-painted with blue paint, then with red.

PAINTING A CHECK DESIGN

For a dramatic check pattern on walls, apply paint with squares of cellulose sponge. For easier application of the paint, glue the sponge to a piece of plywood and use it as a stamp. As a final step, add more dimension and color to the design, if desired, by lightly stamping another paint color over the checks. For this second paint color, use a square stamp of the same size, or make a stamp in a smaller size or shape.

For even rows, the check pattern works best for walls that have squared corners and ceiling lines. A plumb line may be used as a vertical guide. Plan to start painting at the most prominent corner of the room and work in both directions so full squares will meet at that corner. You may want to divide the dominant wall evenly into checks across the width of the wall.

Flat latex or low-luster latex enamel paint may be used for painting walls. To provide a more durable finish on cabinets and furniture, use a gloss enamel. Fabrics may be stamped for coordinating table linens (page 78). For fabric painting, textile paints are used; heat-set the paints according to the manufacturer's directions.

Before you start painting, prepare the surface as on page 39. Practice the technique and test the paint colors on a large piece of cardboard.

Checked cabinet doors (left) are painted using small sponges as stamps. The sponges were cut to size so the finished design fits within the door panel.

MATERIALS

- Latex paint in desired background color, for base coat.
- Latex paint in one or more colors, for stamped design.

- Large cellulose sponges.
- Scraps of ¼" (6 mm) plywood; hot glue gun and glue sticks.
- Thin transparent Mylar® sheets.

1 Cut cellulose sponge into the desired size of square for check design; cut plywood to same size. Make a stamp by securing sponge to plywood, using hot glue. Make one stamp for each color and shape in design.

2 Prepare surface (page 39). Apply base coat of paint in desired background color; allow to dry. Mark placement for first row of design, at bottom of wall, using pencil. For example, for a 3" (7.5 cm) stamp, lightly mark wall at 3" (7.5 cm) intervals. (Pencil markings are exaggerated to show detail.)

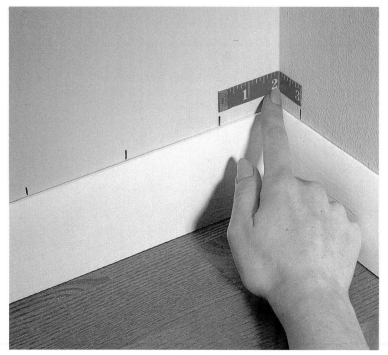

3 Mark wall to corner. If full width of design does not fit into corner, measure around corner, and mark. Then continue marking full widths. Mark spaces on all walls.

4 Lightly mark a plumb line on wall, at the first marking from corner, using a level and pencil. Or hang a string at corner, using a pushpin near top of wall; weight string at bottom so it acts as a plumb line.

5 Apply paint to the sponge, using paintbrush. Stamp the bottom row of checks onto the wall.

6 Continue to stamp rows of checks, working up from bottom of wall and using previous row and plumb line as horizontal and vertical guides. If full stamped design does not fit into corners or at top of wall, leave area unpainted at this time.

7 Allow paint to dry. To fill in areas with partial stamped designs, place a piece of Mylar® over previously painted checks to protect wall. Stamp design up to corners and top of wall, overlapping stamp onto Mylar. Allow paint to dry.

8 Add dimension and color to check design, if desired, using stamp of same size and shape as checks, or cut to a different size and shape. Apply another paint color, stamping very lightly over painted checks. Dispose of used stamps.

WALLCOVERING

Wallcoverings are popular for kitchens, adding pattern or texture to the walls. Use wallcovering throughout the room or on a single wall as a focal point. For the look of wainscoting, wallcover the upper or lower portion of the room and add a wallcovering border for a chair rail effect. Borders can also be used as a trim along the ceiling or as a frame around doors and windows.

SELECTING THE WALLCOVERING & ADHESIVE

Fabric-backed vinyl wallcoverings are an excellent choice, because they are very durable and easily washed. Solid vinyl that has a paper backing is also suitable, but is significantly less durable than the fabric-backed vinyl. Vinyl-coated wallcovering may also be used; although it is also washable, it is less durable than the other vinyls. To keep any wall imperfections from being noticeable, avoid using wallcoverings with a high sheen. For easier installation, select a prepasted wallcovering.

If you are using unpasted wallcovering, you will need to purchase wallcovering adhesive. The type of adhesive varies with the type of wallcovering used, and products also vary from brand to brand. When purchasing the wallcovering, consult the salesperson about the proper adhesive. In addition to the general adhesive used, you will need a seam adhesive for areas where vinyl wallcovering strips overlap, such as around wall corners.

PREPARING THE WALL SURFACE

Wallcoverings adhere only to well-prepared surfaces. Clean the surface to remove any grease or soil. Then rinse it thoroughly with clear water; any detergent left on the wall may prevent the wallcovering adhesive from adhering. Repair any cracks or dents in the wall, filling them with spackling compound or patching plaster so the surface is flat and smooth. Degloss shiny surfaces by sanding them.

It is recommended that you always apply a premixed wallpaper sizing to the surface before you hang the wallcovering, to prevent the adhesives from soaking into the surface.

Turn off the electrical power while working around receptacles and switches. Remove the switch and outlet plates; apply masking tape over the receptacles to keep out any water and adhesive.

REMOVING OLD WALLCOVERING

Loose, peeling wallcovering must be removed before applying the new wallcovering. If the old wallcovering appears sound, you may be able to apply a new layer over it, provided that the previous pattern or color will not show through the new layer.

To remove old wallcovering, wet it down with a sponge, then pull or scrape it off a few minutes later. Place drop cloths on the floor to protect it from water. Wallcovering removers, which may speed the job, are also available in paint and wallcovering stores, although they are messy to use. If the wallcovering is difficult to remove or adheres stubbornly in certain areas, you may want to rent a steamer to remove the wallcovering.

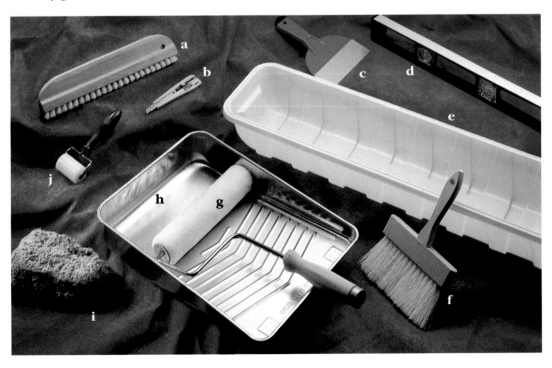

Wallcovering tools include a smoothing brush **(a),** a razor knife with a breakaway blade **(b),** a wide broadknife **(c),** a carpenter's level **(d),** a tray for use with prepasted wallcovering **(e),** a paste brush **(f),** paint roller **(g)** and paint tray **(h),** for applying adhesive to an unpasted wallcovering, a natural sea sponge **(i),** and a seam roller **(j).**

- Wallcovering; measure walls to determine the amount needed.
- Premixed sizing, for preparing the wall surface.
- Premixed adhesive, for unpasted wallcovering.

- Seam adhesive, for securing vinyl wallcovering at the corners.
- Wallcovering tools as listed on page 53.

HOW TO MEASURE & CUT WALLCOVERING STRIPS

1 Hold the wallcovering against the wall. Make sure there is a full pattern at ceiling line. Wallcovering should overlap ceiling and baseboard by about 2" (5 cm). Cut the strip with scissors.

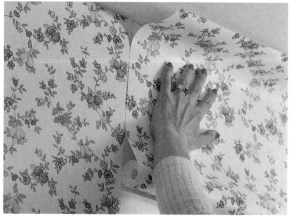

2 Find pattern match for next strip after hanging first strip; then measure and cut new strip.

HOW TO PREPARE WALLCOVERING

1 **Prepasted wallcovering.** Fill water tray half full of lukewarm water. Roll cut strip loosely, adhesive side out. Wet the roll in tray as directed by the manufacturer, usually for about 1 minute.

2 Hold one edge of strip with both hands, and lift the wallcovering from water; check pasted side to make sure strip is evenly wet.

Unpasted wallcovering. Place strip patterned side down on flat surface. Apply adhesive evenly, using paint roller or paste brush. Wipe adhesive from table before preparing next strip.

HOW TO HANG WALLCOVERING

1 Measure from the corner a distance equal to the wallcovering width minus ½" (1.3 cm); mark a point. Draw a plumb line at marked point, using carpenter's level.

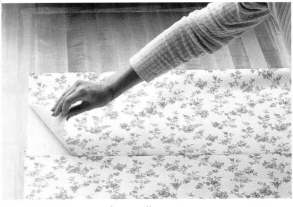

2 Cut and prepare first wallcovering strip, opposite. To *book* the strip, fold ends to center, pasted side in, without creasing folds. Allow the strip to set for about 10 minutes, to cure.

3 Unfold top portion of booked strip. Position the strip lightly on the wall, with edge butted against plumb line; using palms to slide strip in place, overlap strip onto ceiling about 2" (5 cm), with a full pattern repeat at ceiling.

4 Snip top corner of strip so the wallcovering wraps smoothly around corner. Press top of the strip flat with a smoothing brush. Starting at the top, smooth out the wallcovering from center in both directions. Check for bubbles; pull the strip away, and reposition as necessary.

5 Unfold bottom of the strip; use palms to position strip against the plumb line. Press strip flat with smoothing brush; check for bubbles, and reposition as necessary.

6 Hold wallcovering against ceiling or molding with wide broadknife. Trim excess with a sharp razor knife; keep the knife blade in place while changing the broadknife position.

7 Rinse adhesive from wallcovering, using clear water and a sponge; do not run water along edges.

(Continued)

8 Hang next strip so pattern matches, butting edges. Roll seams, using seam roller, after wallcovering has set for ½ hour. Do not press out adhesive.

9 Hang wallcovering over outlets that are covered with masking tape, with electrical power turned off. Make small diagonal cuts to expose outlet. Trim the wallcovering to edges of the opening, using razor knife.

10 **Inside corner.** Cut and prepare a full strip (page 54). While the strip cures, measure from edge of previous strip to inside corner of room at the top, middle, and bottom. Add ½" (1.3 cm) to the longest of these measurements.

11 Cut booked strip from step 10 to this width. Position cut strip on wall, butting edge to previous strip; wrap the strip slightly around corner. Snip the corner at top and bottom; flatten the strip with a smoothing brush, and trim excess.

12 Measure remaining width of strip. Mark the distance from corner onto the uncovered wall; mark a point with pencil. Draw a plumb line at this point from ceiling to floor, using carpenter's level.

13 Position remaining width of strip from step 10 on wall, with the cut edge toward corner and the factory edge against plumb line. Press flat with smoothing brush; trim excess at top and bottom.

14 Peel back the edge at corner, if vinyl wallcovering does not adhere where overlapped. Apply seam adhesive to the lapped seam, if necessary; press flat. Rinse away all excess seam adhesive, using a damp sponge; once dry, it is permanent.

HOW TO HANG WALLCOVERING AROUND WINDOWS & DOORS

1 Position strip on the wall, directly over window frame or door frame. Butt the seam carefully against the edge of the previous strip. Smooth the flat wall areas with a smoothing brush; press strip tightly against casing.

2 Cut diagonally from edge of strip to top corner of frame, using scissors; for a window, repeat at bottom corner.

3 Trim the excess wallcovering to 1" (2.5 cm) from the inside of the frame. Smooth out the wallcovering, pressing out any bubbles.

4 Hold wallcovering against outer edge of frame with a broadknife; trim excess with a sharp razor knife. Trim excess at ceiling and baseboard. Rinse wallcovering and frame, using damp sponge and clear water.

5 Cut and apply short strips for the sections above door or window, matching the pattern; repeat below the window.

6 Position next full strip on wall, with the edge butting the previous strip, matching pattern. Cut diagonally to corners of frame and trim excess at inside of frame as in steps 2 and 3, above.

7 Match seam, below window, on bottom half of strip. Trim excess wallcovering to 1" (2.5 cm) from outer edge of the frame; flatten strip with smoothing brush. Trim excess along bottom of frame, using razor knife and broadknife. Rinse, using a damp sponge.

HOW TO HANG WALLCOVERING BORDERS

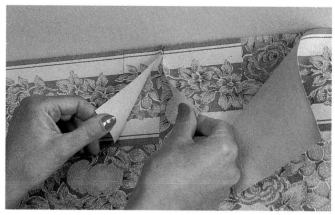

1 Cut and prepare first border strip (page 54); to book strip, fold it accordion-style. Overlap border around corner of adjacent wall for ½" (1.3 cm). Have an assistant hold the booked border while you apply and brush it.

2 Overlap border strips so patterns match, if a seam falls in middle of wall. Cut through both layers with a razor knife. Peel back the border, and remove the cut ends. Press border flat. Roll seam after ½ hour. Rinse, using sponge.

1 Chair rail. Draw a light placement line ¼" to ½" (6 mm to 1.3 cm) below top of chair rail, using a carpenter's level and pencil. Hang wallcovering above this line, if desired. Using a straightedge and razor knife, trim bottom of wallcovering even with placement line.

2 Apply a border strip, with upper edge ¼" to ½" (6 mm to 1.3 cm) above wallcovering; many borders have a stripe that can be visually aligned to the wallcovering, making overlap less noticeable. Press the border flat. If the border does not adhere where overlapped, apply a seam adhesive; press flat. Rinse off all seam adhesive, using sponge.

1 Mitered corners. Apply horizontal border strips, extending them past corners a distance greater than width of the border. Apply vertical border strips, overlapping horizontal strips.

2 Cut through both layers at 45° angle, using a razor knife and a straightedge. Peel back the border; remove ends.

3 Press the border flat. Roll the seam after ½ hour. Rinse, using a damp sponge.

MORE IDEAS FOR WALLCOVERING

Decorative border *is positioned about 2 ft. (0.63 m) below the ceiling to divide the wall.*

Double row of border strips *(left) gives greater impact along the ceiling.*

Coordinating wallcoverings *are used above and below the chair rail border.*

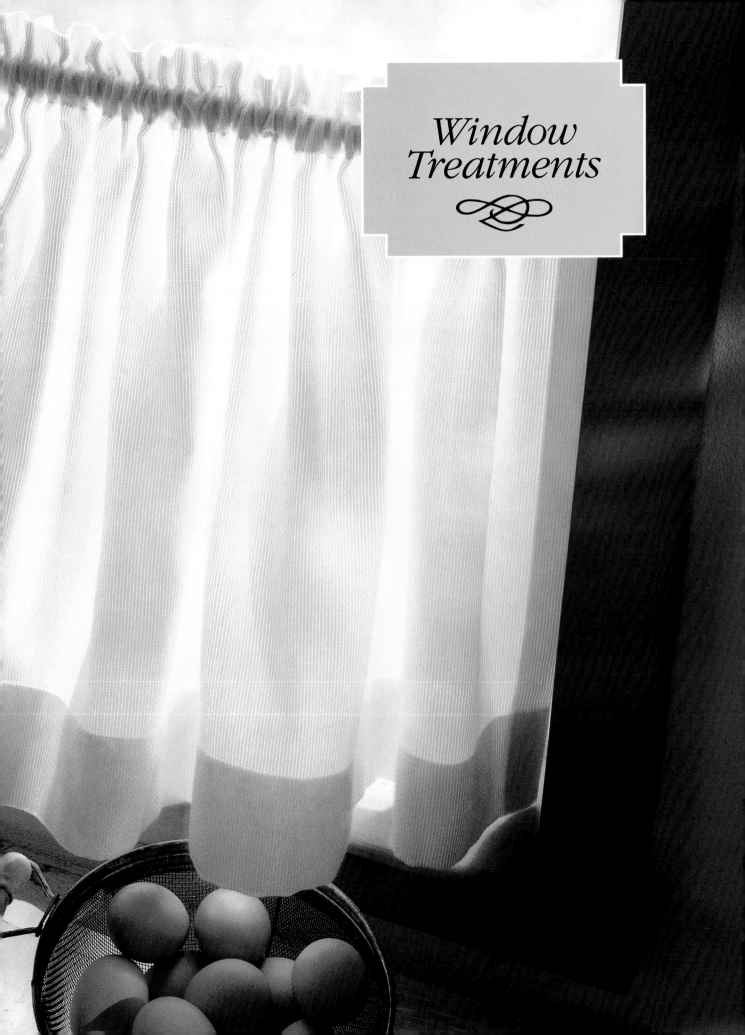

Window Treatments

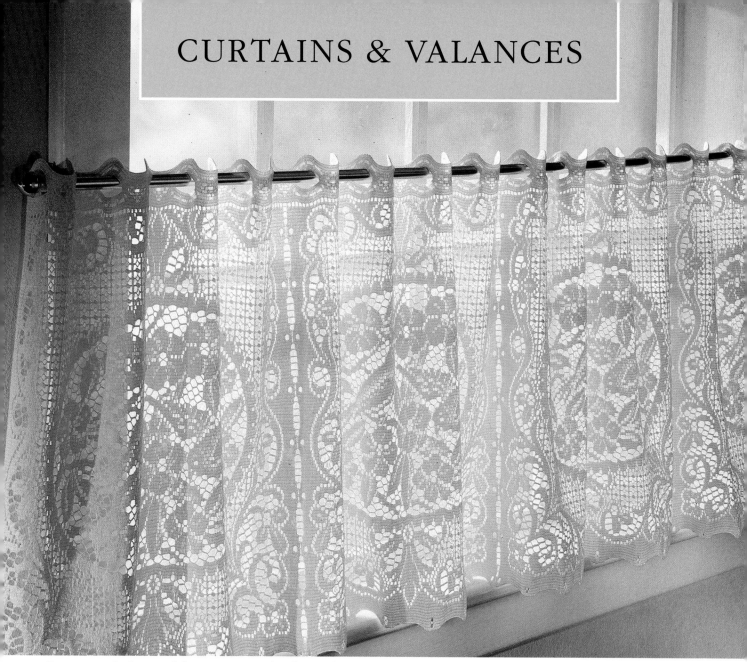

Lace panels *designed for curtains and valances have beading holes at the top, so you can hang them on cafe rods without the need to sew casings.*

Classic cafe curtains and valances are popular window treatments for kitchens. Simple in styling, they are also simple to sew. For a variety of looks, they can be made from fabric, lace panels, or kitchen towels.

Rod-pocket curtains and valances are simply flat panels of fabric, gathered as they are fed onto the curtain rod. When used in kitchens, they are often unlined for a soft, lightweight look.

Lace panels made especially for curtains and valances are the easiest window treatments of all. Depending on the style of the panels, cafe rods are either inserted into prestitched rod pockets or woven in and out of a row of beading, or holes, at the top. Cotton and polyester laces are available in various lengths, some sold as premade panels while others are sold by the yard. To show off the lace design, the cafe curtains are gathered to 1½ times

fullness, so the combined width of the panels measures 1½ times the width of the rod.

For a pouf curtain or valance, weave a ribbon in and out of the lace at intervals of about 12" (30.5 cm) to gather the bottom of the panel. For a pouf valance, gather a 24" (61 cm) panel to a length of 12" to 18" (30.5 to 46 cm). Or the lower portion of a lace panel can be gathered to make a pouf curtain.

Kitchen towels of linen or cotton can become creative cafe curtains for small windows. Whenever possible, take advantage of the existing hems in the towels; if several towels are seamed together for curtain panels, rehem the lower edges for a more finished look. For a layered valance, kitchen towels are overlapped and attached to a mounting board. Determine the length of the board and mount it as on pages 70 and 73.

Kitchen-towel curtains and valance *have a colorful, homespun look.*

Lace pouf valance and matching curtains *are made from purchased panels with prestitched rod pockets. For the pouf valance, the bottom is gathered with ribbons.*

Rod-pocket cafes, *mounted on a wood pole with finials, are a light, airy window treatment.*

WINDOW TREATMENTS

HOW TO SEW ROD-POCKET CAFES & VALANCES

MATERIALS

- Lightweight fabric.
- Curtain rod.

CUTTING DIRECTIONS

Determine the desired finished length of the curtain or valance from the top of the heading to the hemmed lower edge. Also decide on the depth of the rod pocket and heading and the depth of the lower hem. The rod pocket is one-half the measurement around the rod plus ¼" (6 mm); lower hems may be 3" (7.5 cm) for cafes and 2" (5 cm) for a valance. The cut length of the fabric is equal to the desired finished length of the curtain plus the depth of the heading and rod pocket, ½" (1.3 cm) for turn-under at the upper edge, and twice the hem depth.

Determine the cut width of the fabric by multiplying the length of the rod times 2½; if you are sewing two curtain panels, divide this measurement by two to determine the cut width of each panel. For each panel, add 4" (10 cm) to allow for 1" (2.5 cm) double-fold side hems; if it is necessary to piece the fabric widths together, also add 1" (2.5 cm) for each seam.

1 Seam the fabric widths, if necessary, for each curtain panel. At lower edge, press under the hem allowance twice to wrong side; stitch hem.

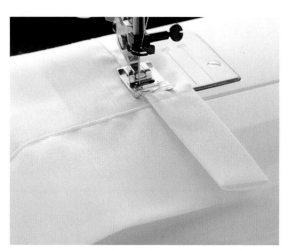

2 Press under 1" (2.5 cm) twice on the sides; stitch the side hems.

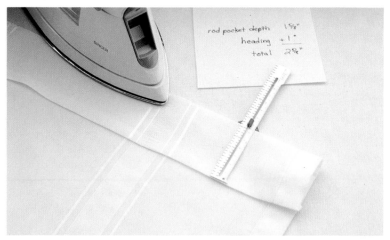

3 Press under ½" (1.3 cm) on upper edge. Then press under an amount equal to rod-pocket depth plus heading depth.

4 Stitch close to first fold. Stitch again at depth of heading, using seam guide or tape on bed of sewing machine as guide for stitching.

5 Insert rod through rod pocket, gathering fabric evenly. Hang curtains.

HOW TO MAKE LACE POUF CURTAINS & VALANCES

MATERIALS

- Lace panels.
- Ribbon.
- Cafe rod.

1 Stitch the side hems, if necessary. Weave ribbon vertically in and out of holes in the lace, at lower portion of panel; tie into a bow. Repeat at intervals of about 12" (30.5 cm).

2 Insert cafe rod into rod pocket or beading holes at top of lace panel. Hang curtain or valance.

HOW TO SEW CAFE CURTAINS FROM KITCHEN TOWELS

MATERIALS

- Kitchen towels.
- Extra-wide bias tape.
- Cafe rod.

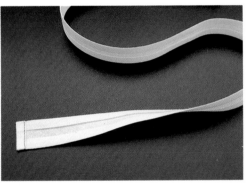

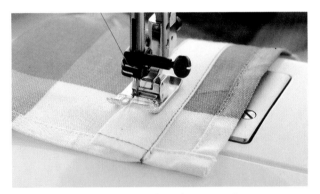

1 Cut a length of extra-wide bias tape for each panel, 1" (2.5 cm) longer than the width of kitchen towel. Stitch narrow hem at each end of bias tape, folding under ¼" (6 mm) twice.

2 Pin bias tape to top of kitchen towel, on wrong side; if heading is desired, place bias tape about 1" (2.5 cm) from upper edge. Stitch along both long edges of bias tape, to make casing. Insert cafe rod; hang curtains.

HOW TO MAKE A VALANCE FROM KITCHEN TOWELS

MATERIALS

- Kitchen towels.
- Mounting board.
- Angle irons.

1 Cut mounting board (page 70). Arrange kitchen towels, and secure to the mounting board, using pushpins; wrap towels around ends of board. Pin the towels together. Draw line on towels even with back edge of board. Trim excess fabric.

2 Remove the valance from board, with the towels pinned together. Stitch towels together; finish raw edges. Reposition the valance on board; staple in place. Mount the valance (page 73).

AWNING VALANCES

The classic style of an awning valance gives the look of a bistro to a traditional kitchen. Its simple lines also make this window treatment suitable for other decorating styles, including contemporary, transitional, and country.

The main body of the awning is constructed from one or more fabric widths with separate pieces for the rod pockets. Although the length of the awning may vary, a suitable length for most windows is 15" (38 cm).

The awning is supported by two curtain rods of equal length. If the awning is used between wall cabinets, a pressure rod is used for the upper rod. Otherwise, a cafe rod is used for the upper rod; to provide a flush mount, the cafe rod is mounted with cup hooks instead of the usual brackets. For the lower rod, a canopy rod with an 8" (20.5 cm) projection is used, to hold the awning away from the window at the bottom.

CUTTING DIRECTIONS

Make the awning pattern as on page 68, steps 1 to 4; cut one awning piece from the outer fabric and one from the lining. For the upper rod pocket, cut one 3¼" (8.2 cm) strip from the outer fabric, with the length of the strip 2" (5 cm) longer than the rod width measurement from step 1. For the lower rod pocket, cut a 2" (5 cm) strip from the lining fabric; the strip is cut to the same width as the lower edge of the awning pattern.

MATERIALS

- Outer and lining fabrics.
- Cafe rod, 1" (2.5 cm) cup hooks, and plastic anchors sized for #4 screws, for upper rod if awning is not mounted between wall cabinets. Or pressure rod, for upper rod if awning is mounted between wall cabinets.
- Canopy rod with 8" (20.5 cm) projection, #4 screws, and plastic anchors sized for #4 screws, for lower rod.
- Drill.
- 5/32" drill bit.

HOW TO MOUNT THE RODS FOR AN AWNING VALANCE

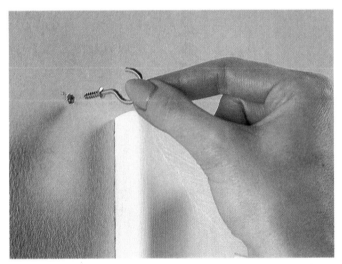

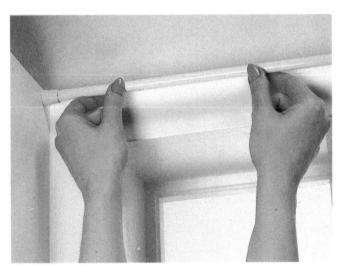

Cafe rod. Mark position for cup hooks about 1" (2.5 cm) outside and above window frame. Unless at wall stud, drill holes for plastic anchors, using 5/32" drill bit. Tap plastic anchors into drilled holes; screw cup hooks into anchors. Repeat to install cup hooks at 36" (91.5 cm) intervals. Hang cafe rod on cup hooks. Lower rod is mounted after awning is sewn.

Pressure rod. Mount a pressure rod between cabinets at top of window, following manufacturer's directions. Lower rod is mounted after awning is sewn.

HOW TO MAKE THE PATTERN FOR AN AWNING VALANCE

1 Measure the distance between outer cup hooks or the distance between the wall cabinets; this is rod width measurement. On tracing paper, draw a line for the lower edge of awning equal to rod width plus 16" (40.5 cm).

2 Draw perpendicular line **(a)** at each end of lower edge, equal to desired length of awning; 15" (38 cm) length works well for most windows. Mark a line **(b)** across width of pattern, 4" (10 cm) above lower edge; this is the drop length.

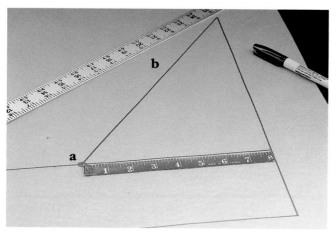

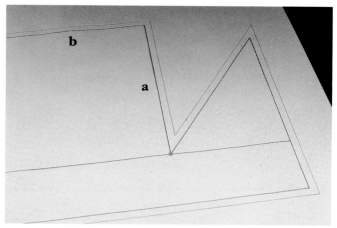

3 Mark a dot **(a)** on marked line for the drop length, 8" (20.5 cm) from each side; this marks the points of darts. Draw line **(b)** from marked dot diagonally to upper end of line for awning length; repeat for other side. Measure length of diagonal line.

4 Draw vertical lines **(a)** of same length as diagonal lines, starting at marked dots. Draw horizontal line **(b)** across top of valance; this should measure same distance as rod width. Add ½" (1.3 cm) seam allowances on all sides.

5 Cut one awning piece from outer fabric and one from lining, piecing fabric widths as necessary. Transfer markings for dart points to wrong sides of the outer fabric and lining. Transfer line for drop length to the right side of lining.

HOW TO SEW AN AWNING VALANCE

1 Press ¼" (6 mm) to wrong side on both long edges of lining strip for lower rod pocket. Turn under 1⅛" (2.8 cm) at ends; stitch. Pin strip to lining, with top of strip along the marked line for drop length and ends of strip ⅝" (1.5 cm) from the side edges. Stitch close to top and bottom of strip.

2 Stitch darts in outer fabric, ½" (1.3 cm) from raw edges, stitching to marked dots. Clip to point of each dart, and trim seam allowances near points; press darts open. Repeat for darts in the lining.

3 Press 1" (2.5 cm) to wrong side at each end of the fabric strip for rod pocket; topstitch in place. Fold fabric strip in half lengthwise, wrong sides together; baste raw edges together.

4 Pin rod pocket to upper edge of the awning piece from outer fabric, with the ends of rod pocket at dart seamlines and the raw edges aligned. Stitch ½" (1.3 cm) seam.

5 Pin outer fabric and lining right sides together; stitch around all edges, leaving 5" (12.5 cm) opening along side. Clip corners. Press lining seam allowances toward lining.

6 Turn the awning right side out; press seamline of rod pocket and edges of awning. Slipstitch opening closed. Fold and press awning along dart seamlines, right side out.

7 Insert rods into rod pockets. Hang awning from upper rod. Mark bracket positions for the lower rod, directly under cup hooks or ends of pressure rod. Install lower rod.

BUTTERFLY SWAGS

Butterfly swags have a simple styling that works well for many decorating schemes. This lined stationary window treatment can be made in any length, from valance length to full length. Its fanfolded fabric is held in place with decorative straps. The folds swag in the center and flare at the sides, creating the butterfly effect.

The swag, attached to a mounting board, may be used alone or over a shade or blinds. If there is no undertreatment, a 1 × 2 mounting board can be used. With an undertreatment, use a mounting board that will project out from the window frame enough so the valance will clear the undertreatment by 2" to 3" (5 to 7.5 cm). The length of the mounting board is equal to the desired finished width of the valance.

The mounting board is installed at the top of the window frame, or just outside it, using angle irons a little shorter than the width of the board. Whenever possible, screw the angle irons into wall studs, using pan-head screws. For a secure installation into drywall or plaster, use molly bolts.

Butterfly swag *can be sewn as a long window treatment (above) for privacy or as a valance (opposite) to enjoy the view.*

MATERIALS

- Decorator fabrics, for swag and straps.
- Lining fabric.
- Mounting board.
- Heavy-duty stapler; staples.
- Angle irons; pan-head screws or molly bolts.

CUTTING DIRECTIONS

The cut length of the swag is equal to the desired finished length at the straps plus 25" (63.5 cm); this allows for the pleats, seam allowance, and mounting. To determine the width of the fabric, add the desired width of the swag plus 1" (2.5 cm) for the two seam allowances at the sides plus twice the width, or projection, of the mounting board. Cut the fabric and lining to this length and width, piecing fabric widths together, if necessary.

For straps with a finished width of 1½" (3.8 cm), cut two straps, 4" (10 cm) wide, with the cut length of the straps equal to twice the desired finished length plus 4" (10 cm); this allows for the mounting and the length taken up across the bottom.

HOW TO SEW A BUTTERFLY SWAG

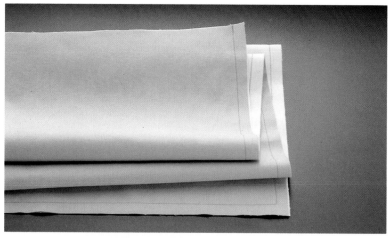

1 Seam fabric widths, if necessary. Place the outer fabric and lining right sides together; pin. Stitch ½" (1.3 cm) seam around sides and lower edge; leave upper edge unstitched.

2 Clip lower corners. Press the lining seam allowance toward lining. Turn swag right side out, and press.

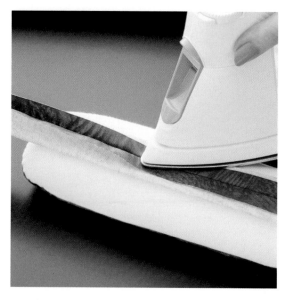

3 Fold one strap piece in half lengthwise, right sides together; stitch ½" (1.3 cm) seam on the long edge. Press seam open with tip of iron, taking care not to crease the fabric. Turn strap right side out, centering seam on back; press. Repeat for the second strap.

4 Determine desired placement for straps, 6" to 10" (15 to 25.5 cm) from end, depending on width of swag. Pin one end of each strap, right side up, to upper edge of swag at desired placement.

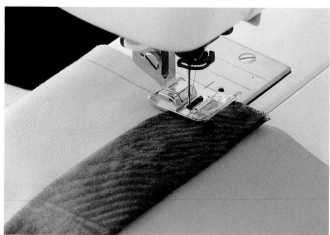

5 Wrap straps under bottom of swag; pin remaining end of each strap in place on lining side of swag, matching raw edges of straps to upper edge of swag.

6 Stitch outer fabric and lining together along the upper edge of swag, securing straps in stitching. Finish raw edges, using zigzag or overlock stitch.

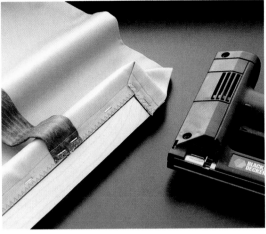

7 Mark lines on top of the mounting board, 1" (2.5 cm) from front and sides. Center swag on board, with upper edge of the swag along the marked line. Staple in place at 2" (5 cm) intervals; apply two staples at each strap.

8 Wrap side of swag around end of the mounting board; staple in place on top of board, along marked line, forming a squared corner. Repeat for remaining side.

9 Secure angle irons to the bottom of the mounting board, near ends and at 45" (115 cm) intervals, using pan-head screws. Secure the angle irons to the top of window frame or to wall, using pan-head screws or molly bolts.

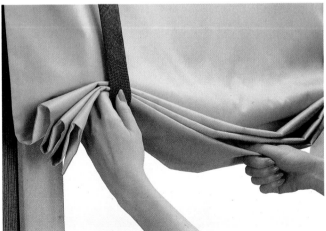

10 Fanfold the lower 24" (61 cm) of swag into five or six pleats, beginning by folding under the lower edge toward the lining.

11 Pull the pleats gently into swagged position at center. Adjust folds as desired near straps.

MORE IDEAS FOR WINDOW TREATMENTS

Stenciled rod-pocket cafes (page 64) are used for this window treatment. Use precut stencils, and follow the manufacturer's instructions for stenciling.

Awning valance (page 67) is teamed with shutters. The shutters are painted with a sprayer as on pages 40 and 41.

Herb garden and ivy decorate this window for a novelty treatment. The ivy is entwined along a peg rail (page 109).

Accessories

TABLECLOTHS & PLACEMATS

Bordered table linens *include the tablecloth above, decorated with a painted check design, and several styles of placemats (opposite), some laminated and painted.*

Tablecloths and placemats with mitered borders have a simple style that works well for decorating kitchens. For more detailing, add fabric painting, like the check design shown here, which coordinates with the check wall design on page 49. By making your own tablecoverings, you can customize the sizes and choose from an unlimited selection of fabrics.

For a tablecloth, measure the table and decide on the desired drop length. A drop length of one-third or two-thirds the table height is attractive; the longer length is more formal. The mitered border may be of any width; the tablecloth above has a 6" (15 cm) border. Placemats may also vary in size. A good finished size for a placemat is 12" × 18" (30.5 × 46 cm), including the border.

For placemats that will be especially practical for everyday use, the fabric may be laminated. To clean the laminated placemats, just wipe them off with a damp cloth and allow them to air dry. Laminate the placemat fabric by using a cool-fuse paper-backed fusible adhesive, such as Heat 'n Bond®, which bonds a two-gauge clear vinyl to the right side of the fabric. Because the cool-fuse adhesive bonds at the silk setting of a dry iron, the vinyl adheres to the fabric without melting. The fabric pieces are laminated as on pages 82 and 83, before the mitered border is stitched.

When making painted and laminated placemats, do not use a decorator fabric that has a stain-resistant or water-resistant finish. These finishes often prevent fabric paints from adhering to the fabric and prevent the fusible adhesives from bonding well, causing a bubbled appearance. Placemats may be painted and then laminated, if desired. The fabric paint does not interfere with the bonding and does not smear.

MATERIALS

• Fabrics in two contrasting colors; for painted or laminated tablecoverings, avoid fabrics with stain-resistant or water-resistant finishes.

• Fabric paints and cellulose sponge to use as an applicator stamp, for painting check design.

• Cool-fuse paper-backed fusible adhesive, two-gauge clear vinyl, and silicone lubricant, for laminating placemat fabric.

CUTTING DIRECTIONS

If you are making laminated placemats, laminate the fabric as on pages 82 and 83 before cutting the pieces to the exact size. For a tablecloth or placemat, cut the middle panel to desired length and width plus ½" (1.3 cm), to allow for ¼" (6 mm) seam allowances. You will need four border strips, with the cut width equal to the desired finished width of the border plus 1¼" (3.2 cm). To determine the length of the border strips, add two times the cut width of the border plus 2" (5 cm) to the cut size of the middle panel; cut two border strips based on the width of the middle panel and two based on the length of the middle panel.

1 Apply painted check design to tablecloth or placemat fabric, if desired (page 82); laminate placemat fabric, if desired (pages 82 and 83). Mark middle panel at center of each side, on wrong side; mark center of each border strip on wrong side.

2 Mark the middle panel at all corners, ¼" (6 mm) from each raw edge, on wrong side of fabric.

3 Pin one border strip to one side of middle panel, right sides together, matching raw edges and centers.

4 Stitch border strip to middle panel in ¼" (6 mm) seam, starting and ending at corner markings.

5 Press seam allowances toward border. Fold the middle panel diagonally at corners, matching raw edges of border strips.

6 Place straightedge along fold; draw stitching line for mitered seam on border, using chalk or water-soluble marking pen.

7 Pin and stitch mitered seam, beginning at raw edge and ending at previous seamline.

8 Trim the seam allowances to ¼" (6 mm); finish seam allowances. Press seam to one side.

9 Hem the outer edges by pressing under 1" (2.5 cm) on each side. Open the corner; fold diagonally so pressed folds match. Press; trim corner. Fold the raw edge under ½" (1.3 cm). Fold again on first foldline; press. Stitch hem.

HOW TO APPLY A PAINTED CHECK DESIGN

1 Cut cellulose sponge into squares of desired size, to use as stamps.

2 Cut fabric pieces for tablecloth or placemat (page 80). Tape fabric pieces to flat surface, within seam allowances.

3 Plan placement of design on fabric pieces, between the seam allowances. Pour a little fabric paint onto a small flat container. Dip sponge into paint. Apply to fabric.

4 Allow the paint to dry. Carefully remove tape from seam allowances of fabric. Heat-set paints, following manufacturer's directions. Laminate fabric pieces for the placemat, if desired (below).

HOW TO MAKE A LAMINATED PLACEMAT

CUTTING DIRECTIONS

Cut fabric pieces at least 1" (2.5 cm) larger than the required sizes for the placemat; cut two-gauge clear vinyl and cool-fuse paper-backed fusible adhesive ½" (1.3 cm) smaller than fabric pieces. The pieces will be trimmed to the correct size after they are laminated.

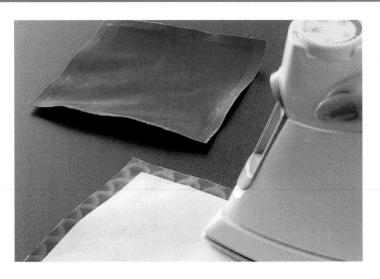

Test the laminating process on scraps of fabric, as in steps 1 to 4, to check the iron temperature and the length of time required for pressing. If the test sample appears milky or the vinyl does not adhere, raise the iron temperature slightly or press for longer time. If sample appears brittle or dry, the iron was too hot or pressing time was too long.

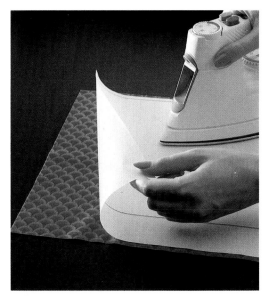

1 Paint a check design on the fabric, if desired (opposite). Center cool-fuse paper-backed fusible web on the right side of the fabric, with the adhesive side down. Fuse, following the manufacturer's directions. Avoid hot iron temperature and a long fusing time; in this step, it is only necessary to secure fabric lightly.

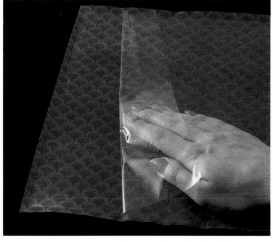

2 Remove paper backing after the fabric has cooled. Place clear vinyl over the fusible adhesive, smoothing out any wrinkles.

3 Cover vinyl with paper backing that was removed, with shiny side of paper against vinyl.

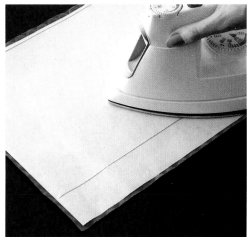

4 Press with dry iron at silk setting for 5 seconds. Lift iron and repeat as necessary until the entire surface is bonded. Save paper backing to use for pressing during construction.

5 Trim all sides of the laminated fabric, trimming pieces to the correct size for placemat.

6 Sew placemat (pages 80 and 81), using paper clips instead of pins to secure the fabric layers and stitching slowly; the seam finishes are not necessary. Topstitch and sew hems from the right side for a smooth appearance at needle holes; apply silicone lubricant to vinyl, to prevent skipped stitches.

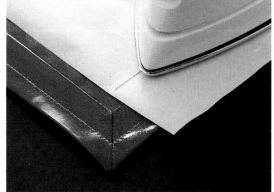

7 Press from vinyl side, using dry iron at silk setting; protect the vinyl by using the paper backing from fusible adhesive as a press cloth. Work quickly, to avoid overpressing. Remove any adhesive residue from right side, using a liquid spot remover or denatured alcohol.

CROSS-STITCHED LINENS

Cross-stitching on linen is easy, and the results are beautiful. This simple craft lends itself to a number of kitchen accessories, including table linens and cafe curtains. On the accessories shown here, latticework is entwined with grapevines. The design (page 86) can be stitched in three different color combinations, for grape clusters of purple, red, and green.

The sewing method of cross-stitching, rather than the usual stab method, is used for linen. With the sewing method, the needle is taken up and down in one stroke, making it faster to stitch on linen than on other fabrics.

Cross-stitch designs are usually stitched over two threads of the linen. To determine the finished size of a design, divide the number of squares in the charted design by one-half the thread count of the fabric.

The centers of the horizontal and vertical rows of the charted design are indicated by arrows. Also indicated by arrows are the points at the ends of the design where the pattern begins to repeat itself; use these indicators when you want to continue to cross-stitch a border of lattice along the lower edge of a curtain panel or around a rectangular placemat.

Although linen is an evenweave fabric, it does have a distinct appearance in the lengthwise and crosswise grainlines. When working on linen, hold the fabric so the selvages run vertically and the crosswise grain runs horizontally. If the selvages have been removed, determine the grainline by pulling out one of the threads in each direction; the crosswise threads are the straightest.

When working with a bright color of embroidery floss that is not colorfast, rinse the skein in cool water until water runs clear, and allow the floss to dry thoroughly. To determine the number of strands of embroidery floss to use, the diameter of the floss to be threaded through the needle should be at least the diameter of one thread pulled from the fabric. Use a blunt-point tapestry needle in a size large enough to be easily threaded with the number of strands of floss you are using; sizes 24 and 26 are commonly used.

MATERIALS

- Linen of desired thread count.
- Embroidery floss in desired colors.
- Blunt-point tapestry needle in size 24 or 26.

Cafe curtains (right) made of linen feature latticework and purple grapes. For the larger design, the stitches are worked over four threads in the linen, using four strands of embroidery floss.

Placemat and napkin (opposite) are made from 32-count linen, worked with two strands of embroidery floss. The lattice design with multicolored clusters of grapes trims one side of the placemat, while a single cluster of red grapes accents a corner of the napkin. Both are finished with narrow hems.

Bread warmer (below) has a cross-stitched corner motif. These grapes are worked in shades of green on 26-count linen, using two strands of floss. For an easy edge finish, machine-stitch ½" (1.3 cm) from the edges and pull the threads from each side to make fringe.

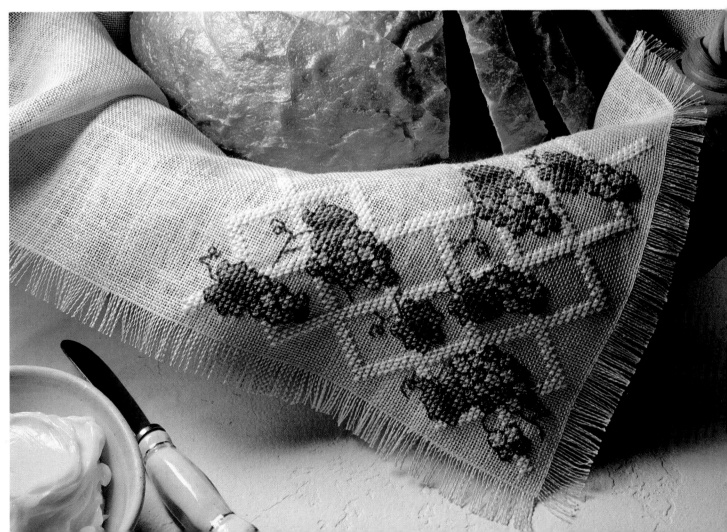

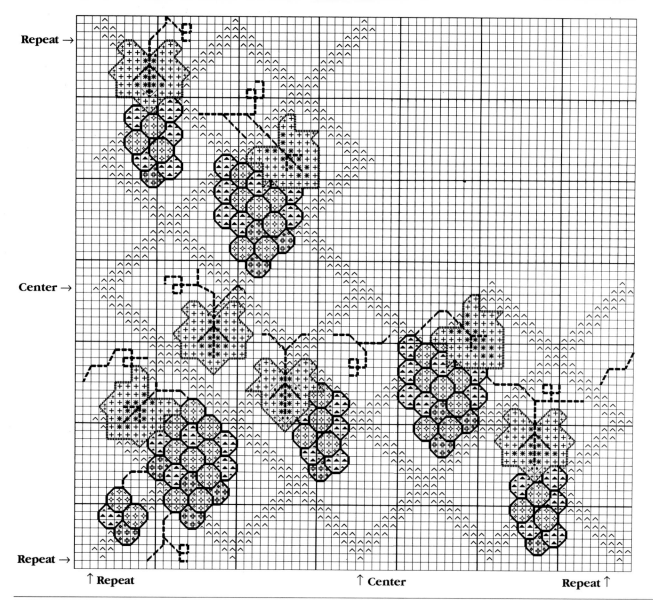

Repeat →

Center →

Repeat →

↑ Repeat ↑ Center Repeat ↑

DESIGN KEY

FOR LATTICE & VINES	FOR GREEN GRAPES	FOR PURPLE GRAPES	FOR RED GRAPES
∧ DMC white.	✧ DMC 472 lt. green.	✧ DMC 554 lt. purple.	✧ DMC 335 lt. red.
+ DMC 988 lt. green.	▲ DMC 471 med. green.	▲ DMC 553 med. purple.	▲ DMC 309 med. red.
✱ DMC 986 dk. green.	✚ DMC 469 dk. green.	✚ DMC 552 dk. purple.	✚ DMC 498 dk. red.
⸱⸱⸱⸱ DMC 986 backstitch.	— DMC 936 backstitch.	— DMC 550 backstitch.	— DMC 814 backstitch.
– – – DMC 300 backstitch.			

TIPS FOR CROSS-STITCHING

Cut the linen so at least 3" (7.5 cm) is allowed on each side of the design. Zigzag around the edges of the linen before you cross-stitch, to prevent raveling.

Fold the fabric in half lengthwise, then crosswise, to find the center; pin-mark. Find this point on the chart, using the arrow guidelines.

Cut embroidery floss into 36" (91.5 cm) lengths, to be folded in half when threading the needle. Separate the strands; recombine the number of strands needed.

Keep the needle 2" to 3" (5 to 7.5 cm) from one end of the floss; if the floss becomes worn next to the needle, it will not be noticeable in the cross-stitching.

Achieve a smoothly stitched surface by crossing all stitches in the same direction.

Skip up to six fabric threads, or three stitches, without breaking the embroidery floss, in order to continue a row of stitches in the same color; do not carry the floss over an area that will remain unstitched.

Unthread the needle to correct mistakes made a few stitches back; pull out the stitches, and restitch them correctly. For larger mistakes, clip the floss to remove the stitches.

Avoid tangling the floss by dropping the needle every few stitches and allowing the floss to untwist.

HOW TO CROSS-STITCH ON LINEN

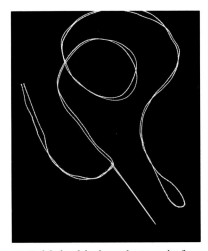

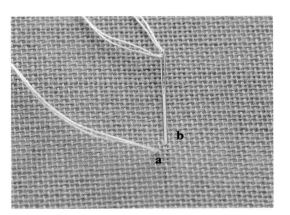

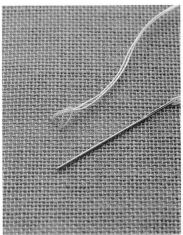

1 Fold double-length strand of embroidery floss in half; thread ends through the needle.

2 Bring the needle up through linen. Make half of the first cross-stitch, beginning **(a)** and ending **(b)** where a vertical linen thread crosses over horizontal thread; this supports stitch on linen. When first stitch is correctly positioned, entire design will be correct.

3 Thread needle through loop on wrong side of linen. Pull floss until loop is snug.

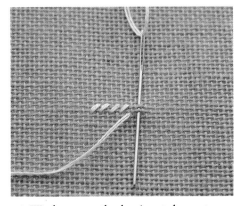

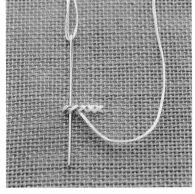

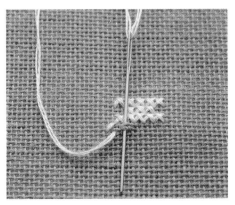

4 Work across the horizontal row to make first half of stitches, working each stitch over two linen threads; in one stroke, insert the needle at top of stitch and bring it up at bottom. Make one stitch for each symbol on chart.

5 Work back over horizontal row to make second half of the cross-stitches, continuing to insert needle at top of stitch and bring it up at bottom.

6 Work rows in a downward direction, to bring the needle down in occupied hole and up in empty hole; this anchors stitches and keeps them smooth. You can turn fabric and chart upside down, if necessary.

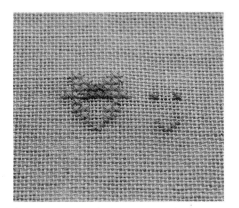

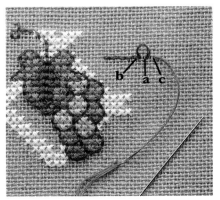

7 Make rounded shapes with one-quarter and three-quarter stitches, as indicated in chart. (Extra stitches were added to show detail.)

8 End stitching for each color or length of floss by bringing floss through to wrong side to complete last stitch. Run floss under several stitches on wrong side. Clip floss close to linen; do not knot floss.

9 Outline details, using backstitch, as indicated on chart and on color key by colored straight lines; make backstitches as shown **(a, b, c).**

CROCHETED RAG RUGS & MATS

Use scraps of fabric to create rugs, placemats, chair seat mats, and trivets. Easy to make with a single crochet stitch, these rugs and mats can be either round or oval. They are so washable, they actually improve with age. Launder them by machine, and lay them flat to dry; for rugs, use a heavy-duty machine.

Use fabrics of 100 percent cotton or cotton blends in solid colors and patterns. For a rug or chair pad, use lightweight to mediumweight fabrics cut into strips 1⅜" (3.5 cm) wide. For a thinner placemat or trivet, use lightweight fabrics cut into 1" (2.5 cm) strips. For a 24" × 36" (61 × 91.5 cm) rug, you will need about 18 yd. (16.56 m) of 45" (115 cm) fabric; for a 13" (33 cm) chair pad, 2½ yd. (2.3 m); for a 12" × 18" (30.5 × 46 cm) placemat, 3¼ yd. (3.0 m); and for an 8" (20.5 cm) trivet, 1 yd. (0.95 m).

The strips are stitched together by machine, then folded and rolled into balls for easier handling during crocheting. For a variegated rug, alternate fabric strips in a single ball. For a more banded look, make a separate ball of each fabric.

To fold the strips quickly and easily, use a bias tape maker, available at fabric stores and from mail-order suppliers. The tape maker automatically folds the strip as you press it.

MATERIALS

FOR THICKER RUGS & CHAIR SEATS

- Lightweight or mediumweight fabric yardage or rags in cotton or cotton blends, cut into 1⅜" (3.5 cm) strips on crosswise or lengthwise grain.
- Size "J" crochet hook and ¾" (2 cm) bias tape maker.

FOR THINNER PLACEMATS & TRIVETS

- Lightweight fabric yardage or rags in cotton or cotton blends, cut into 1" (2.5 cm) strips on crosswise or lengthwise grain.
- Size "I" crochet hook and ½" (1.3 cm) bias tape maker.

Rag rugs and mats, *suitable for many uses, may be either round or oval. The rug and chair mat opposite are thicker than the placemats and the trivet above.*

HOW TO CROCHET A ROUND RAG RUG OR MAT

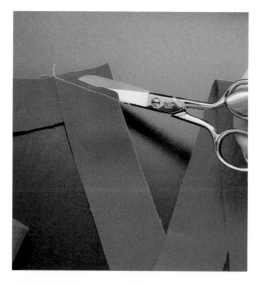

1 Place two strips of fabric, right sides together, at right angles to each other; stitch diagonally across the end, and trim ¼" (6 mm) from stitching. Repeat for several strips of same color or random colors.

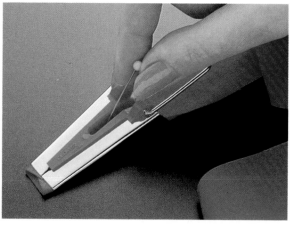

2 Thread fabric strip through channel at wide end of tape maker, bringing strip out at narrow end. Insert pin in slot opening to push strip through.

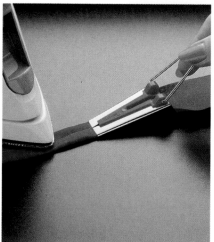

3 Pull fabric through tape maker, to fold raw edges to center of strip; press folds in place.

4 Press strip in half to make double-fold tape; roll into ball.

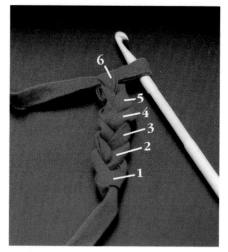

5 Crochet six chain stitches as on page 93, steps 1 to 5.

6 Join chain into a ring with a slip stitch by inserting hook into last chain stitch from hook; pass strip over hook.

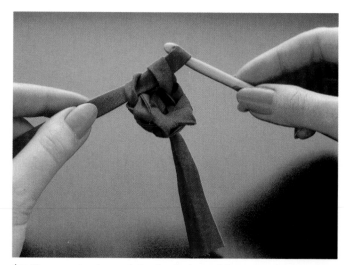

7 Draw strip through both chain and loop in one motion to complete slip stitch.

8 Crochet first round, working single crochet stitches as on page 93, steps 1 to 3; increase in all six stitches of the ring.

9 Stitch the second round, working single crochet stitches by continuing in a spiral and increasing in every other stitch. After the second round, increase as necessary to maintain the shape and flatness of the rug. Increase less often on subsequent rounds.

10 Change colors or add new fabric strips as in step 1, opposite; stitch by machine or by hand.

11 Check flatness of rug often by laying rug on flat surface. If the rug cups, you have not increased often enough; if rug ripples, you have increased too often. Steam-press rug, and remove as many stitches as necessary; then crochet area again to correct the problem.

12 Finish the rug, when the desired size is reached, by trimming the strip narrower, gradually decreasing the width of the strip to ⅜" (1 cm). Refold the strip.

13 End crocheting with a slip stitch by inserting hook into a stitch, with strip over hook; pull strip through stitch and loop in one motion. Cut strip, leaving 8" (20.5 cm) tail. Pull the tail through the loop to secure.

14 Weave end of strip in and out of last round, using crochet hook; repeat for tail at center of rug. Hand-stitch the ends in place, using a needle and hand-sewing thread.

HOW TO CROCHET AN OVAL RAG RUG

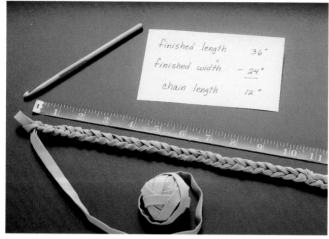

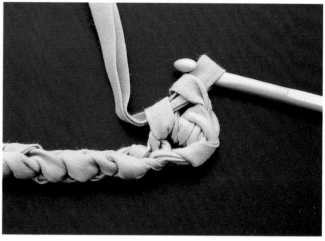

1 Subtract the desired finished width from the desired finished length; crochet a chain of stitches equal to this measurement, as in steps 1 to 5, opposite.

2 Work single crochet stitch in second stitch from hook, and increase, opposite.

3 Single crochet in each stitch of chain to end, without increasing. Single crochet four times in last stitch of chain to increase.

4 Single crochet in each stitch down opposite side of the chain, without increasing. At beginning end of chain, single crochet twice in same stitch as increased in step 2; this gives total of four single crochet stitches in that stitch.

5 Continue to stitch in spiraling rounds, single crocheting each stitch along straight sides; increase as necessary around curved ends to avoid cupping or rippling. Change colors and finish rug as on page 91, steps 10 to 14.

HOW TO MAKE CHAIN STITCHES

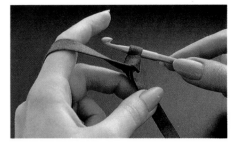

1 Starting. Grasp fabric strip about 2" (5 cm) from the end, between thumb and forefinger. With right hand, lap the long strand over the short one, forming a loop.

2 Hold loop in left hand. Grasp the crochet hook in right hand; insert crochet hook through loop, catching fabric strip.

3 Draw strip through loop; pull loop tight. Lace the strip coming from ball through fingers of left hand and over index finger. Grasp bottom of the loop between thumb and middle finger.

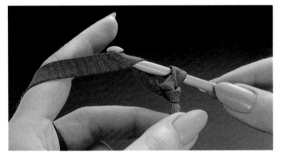

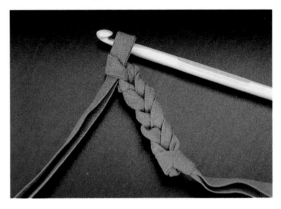

4 Chain stitch. Pass hook under strip. Catch strip with hook, and draw it through loop on hook. This makes one chain stitch.

5 Repeat step 4 until chain reaches desired length or number of stitches. Loop on hook does not count as a stitch. If correct tension is used, chain stitches will be even in size.

HOW TO MAKE SINGLE CROCHET STITCHES

1 Insert the crochet hook under the top two strips from the previous row.

2 Wrap strip over hook, and draw it through chain only, leaving two loops on the hook.

3 Wrap strip over hook again; draw it through both loops on hook, completing one single crochet. When done, one loop is left on hook.

Increasing. Work two single crochets in the same stitch to increase.

RUFFLED STOOL COVERS

Wooden stools make convenient seating at a breakfast nook or counter, either for casual dining or for resting while you prepare food. Padded with foam, this ruffled stool cover adds comfort to a wooden stool.

Ruffled stool covers can be made for stools that are already padded, or the padding can be included in the stool cover. To add padding to the stool cover, use polyurethane foam.

The instructions that follow include a self-lined skirt, which adds body and eliminates the need for a hem. If a heavyweight fabric is used, the skirt may be cut shorter and narrow-hemmed instead.

HOW TO SEW A RUFFLED STOOL COVER

MATERIALS

- Mediumweight fabric; 1½ yd. (1.4 m) is usually sufficient for one stool cover.
- Cording, for welting; 1½ yd. (1.4 m) is usually sufficient for one stool cover.
- Cord, such as pearl cotton, for gathering the ruffle.
- Polyurethane foam, 2" (5 cm) thick.
- Upholstery batting.

CUTTING DIRECTIONS

Make a pattern for cutting the foam by tracing around the top of the wooden stool. Mark a circle this size on the foam; cut the foam, using an electric knife or serrated knife.

For the cover top, cut one circle of fabric, 1" (2.5 cm) larger than the top of the stool, to allow for ½" (1.3 cm) seam allowance.

For the side of the stool cover, cut a boxing strip 1" (2.5 cm) wider than the thickness of the foam, with the length of the boxing strip 1" (2.5 cm) longer than the circumference around the top of the stool.

For a self-lined ruffled skirt with a finished length of 5" (12.5 cm), cut a rectangle of fabric on the crosswise or lengthwise grain, 11" (28 cm) wide by twice the circumference of the stool, piecing the strip, if necessary.

For the welting around the cover top, cut 1½" (3.8 cm) bias strips of fabric, with the combined length of the strips equal to the circumference of the stool top plus 3" (7.5 cm).

For the ties that secure the cover to the legs of the stool, cut eight 2½" × 12" (6.5 × 30.5 cm) fabric strips on the lengthwise or crosswise grain; two ties are used at each leg.

1 Join the bias fabric strips for welting. Fold the strip around the cording, wrong sides together, matching raw edges. Using zipper foot, machine-stitch close to cording.

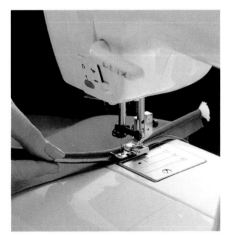

2 Stitch welting to right side of the cover top, over previous stitches on welting, matching raw edges and starting 2" (5 cm) from end of welting; ease welting around curved edge.

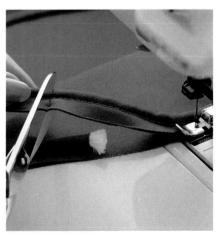

3 Stop stitching 2" (5 cm) from the point where ends of welting will meet. Cut off one end of welting so it overlaps the other end by 1" (2.5 cm).

(Continued)

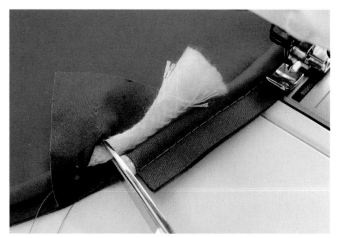

4 Remove the stitching from one end of welting. Trim ends of cording so they just meet.

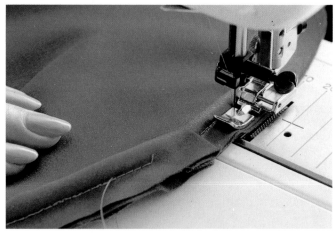

5 Fold under ½" (1.3 cm) of fabric on overlapping end of welting. Lap it around the other end; finish stitching the welting to the cover top.

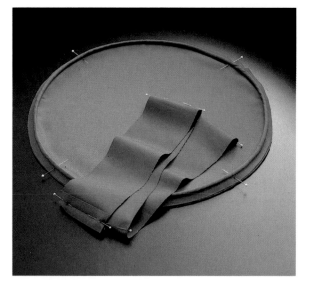

6 Stitch the short sides of boxing strip together, right sides together, in a ½" (1.3 cm) seam; press seam open. Fold the boxing strip into fourths; pin-mark upper and lower edges. Fold cover top into fourths; pin-mark.

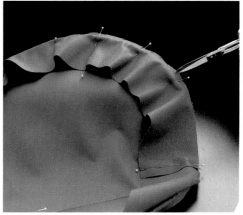

7 Pin upper edge of boxing strip to the cover top, matching pin marks; clip boxing strip within seam allowance as necessary, and ease boxing strip to fit.

8 Stitch boxing strip to the cover top in ½" (1.3 cm) seam, taking care to avoid stitching any tucks; stitch with cover top facing up.

9 Stitch the skirt pieces together in ½" (1.3 cm) seams, right sides together; stitch ends together, forming continuous strip. Press seams open.

10 Fold skirt in half lengthwise, wrong sides together; press.

11 Zigzag over a cord, a scant ½" (1.3 cm) from the raw edges of the skirt.

12 Fold skirt into fourths; pin-mark. Align upper edge of skirt to the lower edge of boxing strip, matching pin marks; gather to fit by pulling on the cord. Pin in place, matching raw edges; stitch ½" (1.3 cm) seam.

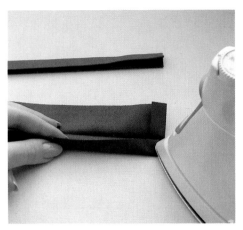

13 Fold ½" (1.3 cm) to wrong side at one end of tie. Press the tie in half lengthwise, wrong sides together. Fold each edge to the center; press. Refold at center; press. Repeat for remaining ties.

14 Stitch along folded lengthwise edge of tie and across folded end.

15 Divide ruffle seam into fourths; pin-mark. Pin two ties to ruffle at each pin mark; align unfinished ends of ties to raw edge of ruffle. Stitch the ties in place along seamline. Finish seam at lower end of boxing strip, using zigzag or overlock stitch. Omit step 16 if purchased stool has padded seat.

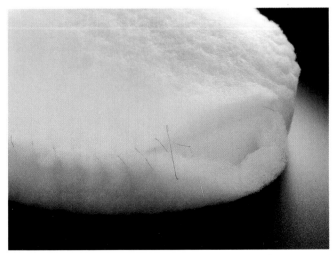

16 Cover the foam with a layer of upholstery batting; hand-baste batting in place. Place foam into cover.

17 Place the cover on the stool with ties at legs of stool. Secure the ties around legs.

UPHOLSTERED CHAIR SEATS

The worn upholstery and padding of kitchen chair seats can be replaced quickly and easily. Even if the seats are not worn, replacing the fabric to coordinate with other furnishings is a quick way to redecorate.

The padded wooden seats of kitchen and dining-room chairs can often be removed by loosening the screws on the underside of the seat. If the foam and batting on the seats are flattened or uneven, they should be replaced to return the seats to a like-new condition. If the existing foam and batting are still in good condition, it is not necessary to remove them.

The instructions that follow are for removable wooden seats with a simple pullover-style of upholstery, often referred to by upholsterers as a slip seat. If additional detailing is desired, welting can be applied to the bottom of the seat by stapling it in place.

HOW TO UPHOLSTER A CHAIR SEAT

MATERIALS

- Decorator fabric; 2 yd. (1.85 m) is sufficient for four chair seats.
- Polyurethane foam, 1" (2.5 cm) thick.
- 3 yd. (2.75 m) polyester upholstery batting, 27" (68.5 cm) wide, for four chair seats.
- Cording, 5⁄32" (3.8 mm) diameter, for welting.
- 2 yd. (1.85 m) cambric or muslin, for underside of four chair seats, optional.
- Foam adhesive.
- Heavy-duty stapler (electric stapler is recommended); 3⁄8" (1 cm) staples.

CUTTING DIRECTIONS

Cut the fabric 6" (15 cm) larger than the length and width of the chair seat. Cut the foam 1" (2.5 cm) larger than the length and width of the chair seat. Cut the cambric or muslin 2" (5 cm) larger than the chair seat.

For the welting at the bottom of the chair seat, cut fabric strips 1½" (3.8 cm) wide on either the bias or the crosswise grain; the combined length of the strips is equal to the distance around the chair seat plus extra for a 2" (5 cm) overlap and for seam allowances.

1 Remove screws on underside of seat; remove seat.

2 Strip off existing fabric, removing staples or tacks with screwdriver and needlenose pliers.

3 Apply spray adhesive to one side of foam; affix the foam to the top of the seat.

(Continued)

4 Place upholstery batting on table, with seat upside down over it. Wrap batting around top and sides of seat. Trim excess batting even with bottom edge of seat.

5 Mark the center of each side on bottom of seat. Notch the center of each side of fabric. Place fabric on table, wrong side up. Center the seat upside down on fabric.

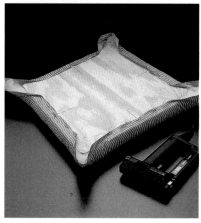

6 Staple fabric to bottom of seat at center back, matching center marks. Stretch fabric from back to front; staple at center front, matching the center marks. Repeat at center of each side.

7 Apply staples to back of seat at 1½" (3.8 cm) intervals, working from center toward sides, to within 3" (7.5 cm) from corners of seat.

8 Pull fabric taut toward front of seat; staple fabric to front as in step 7. Repeat for sides of seat.

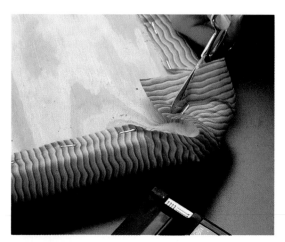

9 Fold fabric diagonally at corner; stretch the fabric taut, and staple between screw hole and corner. Trim excess fabric diagonally across the corner.

10 Miter fabric at corner by folding in each side up to corner; staple in place. Repeat for remaining corners. Trim excess fabric, exposing screw holes. If welting is not desired, omit steps 11 to 15; if cambric is not desired, omit step 16.

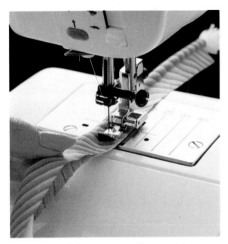

11 Join fabric strips for welting. Fold strip around the cording, wrong sides together, matching raw edges. Using zipper foot, machine-stitch close to cording.

12 Staple welting around seat at ¾" (2 cm) intervals, starting at back of seat 2" (5 cm) from the end of the welting; align stitching line of welting to edge of seat.

13 Stop stapling 3" (7.5 cm) from first staple. Cut off one end of welting so it overlaps the other end by 1" (2.5 cm).

14 Remove the stitching from one end of welting. Trim ends of cording so they just meet.

15 Fold under ½" (1.3 cm) of fabric on the overlapping end of welting. Lap it around the other end; finish stapling welting to chair seat.

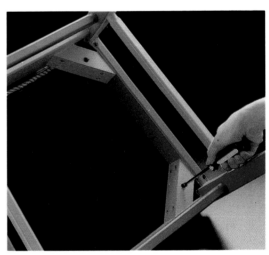

16 Fold under raw edges of cambric or muslin; staple to bottom of the seat at 1" (2.5 cm) intervals. Puncture cambric at screw holes in the chair seat.

17 Screw the upholstered seat to the chair.

HERBAL WALL HANGINGS

An herbal wall hanging is both pretty and practical. This ladder-style wall hanging is constructed from twigs and raffia. Flowering herbs, whole garlic cloves, red pearl onions, and red chili peppers add color and character to the arrangement.

Dried herbs, available from floral and craft stores, are also used for this wall hanging. To dry fresh herbs from your own garden or from the grocery store, bundle them, and hang them upside down in a dark, dry room.

Variation *of the wall hanging substitutes pomegranates, mushrooms, and sections of artichokes for the items in step 4. Heads of wheat and seed pods are added with the dried herbs in step 5.*

HOW TO MAKE AN HERBAL WALL HANGING

MATERIALS

- Dogwood or other twigs.
- Raffia.
- 10 to 12 whole garlic bulbs; 18 to 20 red pearl onions; 10 to 12 dried red chili peppers.

- Dried herbs, such as sage, oregano, lemon balm, lavender, and yarrow, or other dried herbs as desired.
- Floral wire; wire cutter.
- Hot glue gun and glue sticks.

1 Tie four 2" × 11" (5 × 28 cm) bundles of twigs with floral wire; leave 4" (10 cm) tails of wire.

2 Cut a bundle of raffia into 4-ft. (1.27 m) length. Attach raffia to twigs, using tails of wire from bundles; space bundles of twigs 8" to 10" (20.5 to 25.5 cm) apart. Leave excess raffia at bottom of wall hanging.

3 Wrap short lengths of raffia around branches, crisscrossing raffia in front and back; tie. This holds branches more securely and conceals wire.

4 Secure garlic bulbs, pearl onions, and red chili peppers to raffia and twigs, at intersections of the ladder, using hot glue.

5 Secure dried herbs to raffia, using hot glue, spacing the herbs evenly along sides of ladder. Fresh items in wall hanging will dry naturally.

FLOWER BOXES

Boxes filled with an abundance of flowers are a cheerful addition to any kitchen. These flower boxes are fast and easy to construct. The boards are simply butted together and nailed, with strips of corner molding glued in place at the top and corners for a finished look.

The flower boxes can be made in any size. In the instructions that follow, cutting directions are included for a large box that accommodates three 6" (15 cm) clay pots and a small box that accommodates three 4" (10 cm) pots.

The flower boxes may be painted or stained to complement the kitchen decorating scheme. You may choose to finish them using one of the decorative paint finishes on pages 40 to 51.

MATERIALS

- 1 × 8 aspen or maple board, 7 ft. (2.17 m) in length, for large flower box; or 1 × 6 board, 6 ft. (1.85 m) in length, for small flower box.
- 8-ft. (2.48 m) length of 1⅛" (2.8 cm) corner molding for large or small flower box.
- 1¼" 3d finish nails; nail set; wood glue.
- Miter box and backsaw.
- Paint or stain, for desired wood finish.

CUTTING DIRECTIONS

For a large flower box, cut two 7¼" × 22½" (18.7 × 57.3 cm) pieces from 1 × 8 board, for front and back pieces. Also cut two 7¼" × 7¼" (18.7 × 18.7 cm) sides pieces and one 7¼" × 21" (18.7 × 53.5 cm) bottom piece.

For small flower box, cut two 5½" × 16½" (14 × 41.8 cm) pieces from 1 × 6 board, for front and back pieces. Also cut two 5½" × 5½" (14 × 14 cm) side pieces and one 5½" × 15" (14 × 38 cm) bottom piece.

Flower boxes *can be made in various paint finishes. For traditional decorating, the small box above is painted in white enamel. For a country kitchen, the large box opposite has a farmhouse finish (page 46); for the lettering, use precut stencils and aerosol paint.*

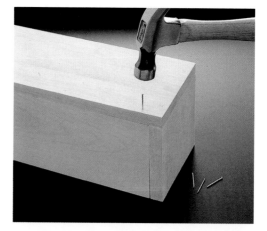

2 Align the bottom piece to the front and side pieces. Drilling through front of box into bottom piece, predrill holes for nails at 4" (10 cm) intervals. Secure with nails.

1 Align one front piece to one side piece as shown. Drilling through front of box into the side piece, predrill two holes for nails about 1" (2.5 cm) deep, using 1/16" drill bit. Secure pieces with nails. Repeat for remaining side piece.

3 Align back piece to the sides and bottom. Drilling through back of box into the side and bottom pieces, predrill holes and secure with nails.

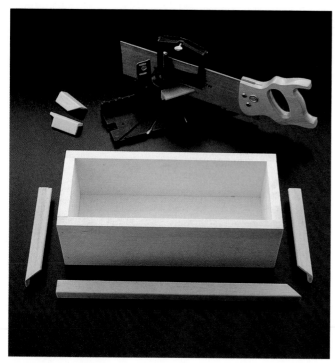

4 Miter moldings for sides of box at front corners; leave excess length on the molding strips. Miter one corner on the molding for front of box, leaving excess length.

5 Position mitered front and side molding strips at one corner. Mark finished length of front piece; mark the angle of the cut. Cut miter.

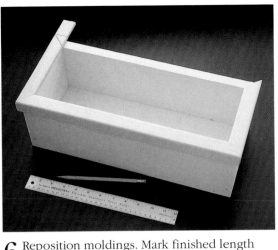

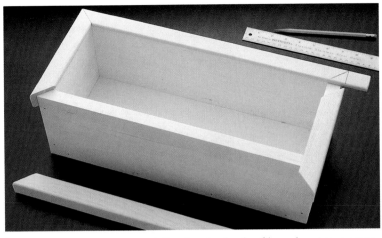

6 Reposition moldings. Mark finished length and angle of cut for side pieces; miter.

7 Miter one corner on molding for the back of box, leaving excess length. Position with side strip; mark finished length. Cut miter.

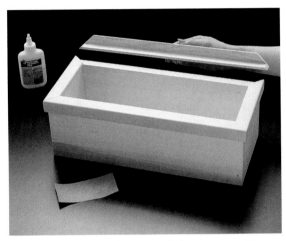

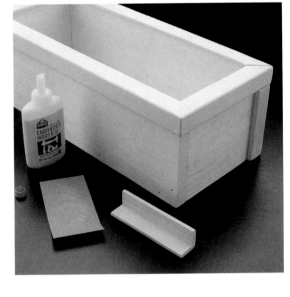

9 Measure from lower edge of the molding to the bottom of box; cut pieces to fit all four corners. Sand the cut edges. Glue moldings in place at the corners.

8 Reposition moldings; sand the corners, if necessary, for proper fit. Glue moldings around top of box, using wood glue.

10 Set the nails at the bottom of box, using nail set. Stain or paint flower box as desired, filling the nail holes with paint or with putty to match stain. Apply clear acrylic finish, if desired.

PLATE RAILS
& PEG RAILS

Plate rails and peg rails are classic kitchen accessories. Both can be conveniently used for storage, perhaps holding wicker baskets and trays, or for displays of collectibles.

PLATE RAILS

Whether you have a few special plates or a large collection, plate rails offer a perfect solution for showing them off, along with a selection of cups and saucers or other serving pieces.

In order to display plates, glue a strip of quarter-round molding to the top of the shelf as on page 110. The molding acts as a stop to keep plates upright and eliminates the need for using a router to groove the shelf. Cove molding can also be secured to the side and front edges of the shelf for added detailing.

Often high on the wall, plate rails are supported on decorative wooden shelf brackets, available in several styles; the brackets include keyholes or hardware for hanging. Place shelf brackets up to 12" (30.5 cm) from the ends of the shelf. On long shelves, use one or more additional brackets, placing them at intervals of 4 ft. (1.27 m) or less.

PEG RAILS

Peg rails, usually chosen for country decorating, also work well in transitional kitchens as a reminder of days gone by. Both decorative and functional, peg rails can serve as a rack for commonly used cooking utensils or be used for displaying bunches of dried herbs.

To make your own peg rail, simply drill evenly spaced holes along the length of a board, and glue premilled pegs into the holes. Then paint or stain the peg rail as desired. You may want to consider a timeworn paint finish, such as the crackled finish on page 42 or the farmhouse finish on page 46.

Whenever possible, mount the peg rail at wall studs. If it is necessary to mount it between studs into drywall or plaster, use molly bolts. Use button plugs to conceal the screw heads.

To eliminate most of the work, use the peg rail molding that is available at woodworking stores and from mail order. This molding has predrilled holes at 8" (20.5 cm) intervals, sized to accommodate premilled pegs. Several styles of pegs are available for use with either a molding you have drilled yourself or a purchased peg rail molding.

HOW TO MAKE & HANG A PLATE RAIL

MATERIALS

- 1 × 8 board of desired length for shelf.
- Decorative shelf brackets.
- ¾" (2 cm) or 1" (2.5 cm) cove molding or other trim molding, for front and side edges of shelf.
- ¼" (6 mm) quarter-round molding, for plate stop.
- Wood glue.
- Molly bolts with screws, one for each shelf bracket.
- 4-ft. (1.27 m) carpenter's level.
- 17 × 1" (2.5 cm) brads.
- Paint or stain as desired.

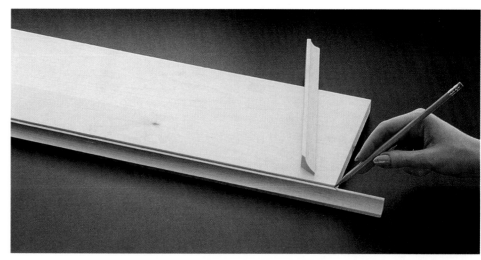

1 Miter molding strips for the sides of 1 × 8 board at front corners; leave excess length on moldings. Miter one corner on molding strip for the front of shelf, leaving excess length; mark finished length and angle of miter cut at opposite end. Cut the miter.

2 Reposition the front and side molding strips at one corner. Mark the finished lengths of the side pieces for straight-cut ends at back edge of shelf.

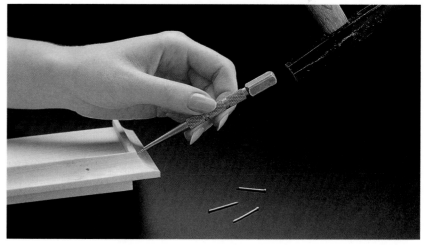

3 Apply glue sparingly to bottom and mitered ends of the molding strips. Position strips on shelf so upper edge of molding extends ¼" (6 mm) above top of shelf; lower edges may not align. Predrill nail holes with ¹⁄₁₆" drill bit. Secure with brads; set brads, using nail set.

4 Cut quarter-round molding to fit the length of the shelf between edge moldings. Apply wood glue to the bottom of quarter-round; secure to top of shelf, positioned 2" (5 cm) from the back edge. Clamp in place, using scrap of lumber to protect plate rail; allow glue to dry for 1 hour.

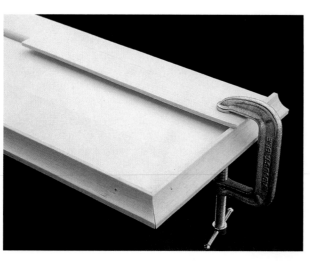

5 Paint or stain the shelf and the brackets as desired.

6 Position one bracket on the wall to the height desired; mark the placement for screw hole.

7 Mark wall with short vertical line at the desired distance for the next shelf bracket.

8 Place the level at marking for first bracket; slide opposite end of the level up and down until it is leveled; mark across placement line for the second bracket to indicate the exact screw placement.

9 Drill holes for molly bolts into wall at placement marks. If there is a wall stud at a placement mark, use a screw rather than a molly bolt.

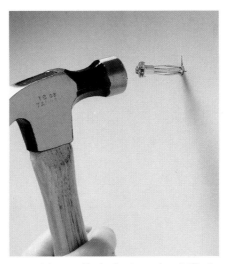

10 Tap molly bolts into the drilled holes, using hammer.

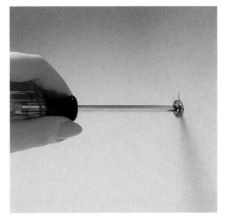

11 Tighten screws, which causes molly bolts to expand in the wall and prevents them from pulling out; then back out the heads ¼" (6 mm) from the wall to receive the bracket. At wall stud, insert screw into drilled hole without molly bolt.

12 Secure decorative brackets to wall screws by sliding keyhole hangers of brackets onto heads of screws.

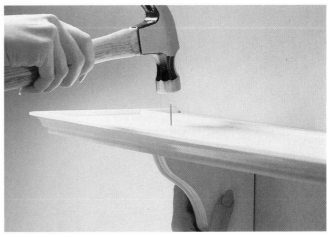

13 Place shelf on brackets. If desired, secure the shelf to brackets, using one flat-head screw or one brad for each bracket.

HOW TO MAKE & HANG A PEG RAIL

MATERIALS

- 3½" (9 cm) molding or 1 × board.
- Premilled pegs.
- Molly bolts and screws.
- Brad-point drill bit, for drilling peg holes.
- ⅛" combination drill and countersink bit, for drilling screw holes.
- Wood glue; 220-grit sandpaper.
- Button plugs, for plugging ⅜" (1 cm) screw holes.
- 4-ft. (1.27 m) carpenter's level.

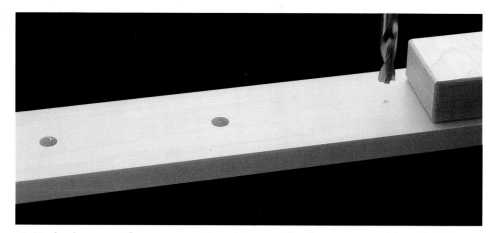

1 Mark placement for pegs, spacing them evenly along center of board. Using drill bit, drill holes at placement marks; use block of wood as a visual guide for vertical holes, keeping drill bit parallel to corner of block.

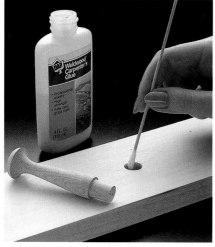

2 Sand the board and pegs smooth. Apply wood glue into the holes sparingly, using cotton swab.

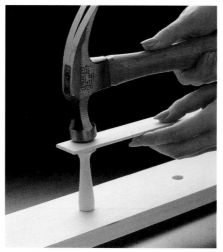

3 Tap pegs into holes, using hammer; place a scrap of lumber on peg, to prevent damage from hammer.

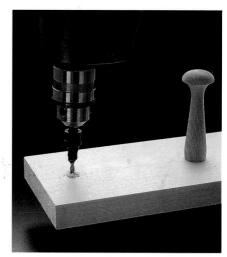

4 Drill holes for screws into ends of peg rail, using ⅛" combination drill and countersink bit.

5 Paint or stain the peg rail and button plugs as desired.

6 Position peg rail on wall to the height desired; tap small nail into wall through one screw hole.

7 Place the level along top edge of peg rail. With the nail holding peg rail at one end, slide the opposite end up and down until peg rail is leveled. Mark placement for screw at the opposite end, using nail.

8 Drill holes for molly bolts into wall at the placement marks. If there is a wall stud at placement mark, molly bolt is not needed.

9 Tap molly bolts into the drilled holes, using hammer.

10 Tighten screws; molly bolts expand in wall, preventing them from pulling out.

11 Remove screw from molly bolt; insert screw into hole of peg rail. Align screw with the installed molly bolt. Screw the peg rail securely in place. At wall stud, insert screw into peg rail, then into a drilled hole without molly bolt.

12 Tap button plugs into holes of peg rail, to conceal screws. Secure each plug with dot of glue, if necessary.

These versatile shelves have simple styling and can be easily built from stock lumber. Custom-sized for your needs, the U-shaped shelves can be hung on the wall or be turned upside down and stacked on the counter. Add a dowel at the front of the shelves, if desired, for more secure storage of jars.

U-shelves can be built from any width of 1 × lumber. If you are not adding a dowel to the shelf, omit steps 1 and 2 in the following instructions.

MATERIALS

- 1 × lumber.
- Sanding block; 80-grit and 220-grit sandpaper.
- 1⅝" (4 cm) drywall screws.
- ⅜" (1 cm) dowel, for plugs and optional front bar.
- Wood glue; awl; chisel.
- ⅜" drill bit; ⅛" combination drill and countersink bit; ⅝" brad-point or Forstner drill bit.
- Jigsaw, circular saw, or backsaw and miter box.
- Coping saw or other small saw.
- Hangers with included screws; two pan-head screws, to mount shelf on a wall.

CUTTING DIRECTIONS

Use a circular saw, jigsaw, or backsaw to cut the lumber for the sides and the bottom of the shelf; a miter box is helpful for use with a backsaw, to achieve straight right-angle cuts. The side and bottom pieces can be cut to any desired lengths. For a spice rack, also cut one ⅜" (1 cm) dowel ⅞" (2.2 cm) longer than the bottom piece. Sand the cut ends of the side and bottom pieces, using a sanding block.

Stacked shelves (left), made from different widths of lumber, are painted with a farmhouse finish (page 46).

U-shelf turned upside down helps to organize the interior cabinet space for stacks of dinnerware.

Spice racks with dowels (below), are hung conveniently near the cooking area.

HOW TO MAKE A U-SHELF

1 Mark the dowel placement ½" (1.3 cm) from inside front edge of each side piece, with the marking 2½" (6.5 cm), or desired distance, from the bottom; using awl, center-punch holes at markings. Using ⅜" drill bit, drill holes for dowel to ½" (1.3 cm) depth; use masking tape on drill bit as guide for the depth.

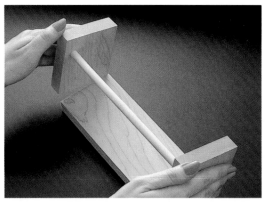

2 Cut dowel ⅞" (2.2 cm) longer than bottom piece; this allows ⅛" (3 mm) clearance between drilled holes. Sand dowel smooth. Sand ends, if necessary, to fit into holes. Insert dowel into holes; test-fit pieces with bottom.

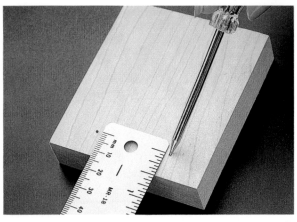

3 Mark location for two screws on the outer side of each side piece, ½" (1.3 cm) from bottom and ¾" (2 cm) from front and back edges. If board is wider than 5" (12.5 cm), also mark a third center hole, ½" (1.3 cm) from bottom. Sand pieces on sides that will be inside shelf.

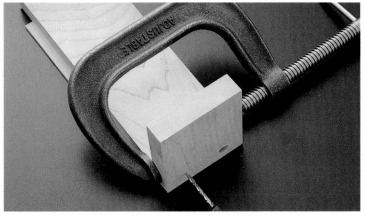

4 Place one side piece upright against the end of bottom piece, with ⅛" (3 mm) spacer under bottom piece; clamp together. Drill 2" (5 cm) holes at markings, through side piece and into bottom piece, using ⅛" combination drill and countersink bit. Insert 1⅝" (4 cm) drywall screws.

5 Insert dowel. Drill holes and insert screws into remaining side as in step 4.

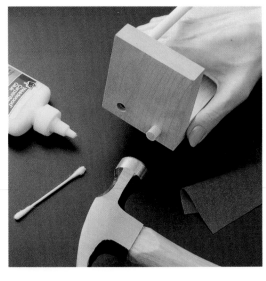

6 Cut ½" (1.3 cm) piece of doweling for each screw hole, for plugs. To bevel one end of each plug, sand or file edge slightly. Apply a small amount of wood glue into holes, using cotton swab. Tap the plugs into holes as far as possible, using hammer or wooden mallet. Wipe any excess glue, using a dampened wool cloth. Allow to dry overnight. If making a wall shelf, follow steps 7 to 10 for hangers while glue dries.

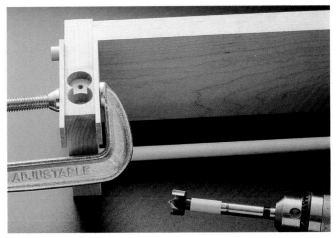

7 Mark position for hangers on back of side pieces, ⅝" (1.5 cm) from upper edge; center hole at top of hanger on mark. Inserting pencil in hole at bottom of the hanger, mark placement for the screw hole. Center-punch at both markings, using awl.

8 Clamp a piece of scrap wood to both sides of the side piece. Using ⅝" brad-point or Forstner drill bit, drill hole for top of hanger to ½" (1.3 cm) depth. Using same drill bit, drill hole at marking for screw to ³⁄₁₆" (4.5 mm) depth, or to depth necessary to recess head of screw.

9 Mortise the hole to accommodate shape of hanger, by squaring it with a small chisel.

10 Drill hole for screw, so depth of hole is longer than length of screw. Insert screw to secure hanger.

11 Cut off excess plugs after glue has thoroughly dried, so plugs extend slightly; use small saw, and take care not to scratch wood surface.

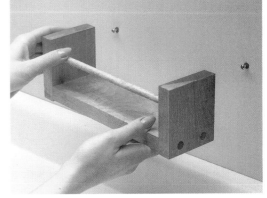

12 Sand the plugs flush with the surface, using an 80-grit sandpaper on sanding block. Sand the exterior of shelf, using fine sandpaper; bevel edges slightly. Paint shelf as desired (pages 40 to 47). Or stain shelf, and apply clear acrylic finish.

13 Measure distance from center of hanger to center of hanger. Insert the pan-head screws into wall, allowing heads of screws to protrude ½" (1.3 cm) from wall surface. Hang shelf on screws.

LATTICE
SHELVES

To accent a kitchen wall, lattice shelves are a fresh, clean accessory. In the shelf shown here, the lattice makes a perfect backdrop for an abundance of ivy in a traditional or French country kitchen. For multiple-shelf variations, try one of the lattice shelves on page 123; the longer, leaner look of the stained shelf is especially suitable for transitional or contemporary decorating.

More of a craft project than a woodworking project, the latticework is simply constructed by arranging the laths and gluing them together, with short lengths of lath used as spacers between the lattice strips. After the glue has set overnight, screw the shelf brackets to the latticework and glue the shelf in place on the brackets.

MATERIALS

- Seven 1⅜" (3.5 cm) pine laths, each 8 ft. (2.48 m) in length.
- Two wooden shelf brackets of pine or maple.
- ¾" (2 cm) cove molding, 5 ft. (1.59 m) in length.
- One 1 × 8 aspen, pine, or maple board, 3 ft. (0.95 m) in length, for shelf.
- Aerosol paint in white or other desired color.
- Two swivel-type hangers, available from frame shops and woodworking stores; 6 × 1" (2.5 cm) brass wood screws.
- Two 8 × 1¼" (3.2 cm) wood screws; wire nails.
- 220-grit sandpaper.
- Wood glue.

CUTTING DIRECTIONS

For lattice strips, cut the lath into two 23" (58.5 cm) lengths, eight 24½" (62.3 cm) lengths, one 11¾" (30 cm) length, one 22⅝" (57.5 cm) length, five 27¾" (70.5 cm) lengths, and two 9¼" (23.6 cm) lengths.

For spacers, cut the lath into 19 lengths, 10" (25.5 cm) each. Also cut four 3¼" (8.2 cm) spacers; these must be cut accurately.

HOW TO MAKE A LATTICE SHELF

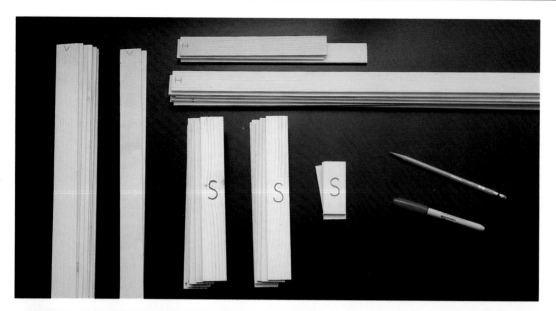

1 Sand the laths smooth. Using a pencil, mark the letter V on right side of all 23" (58.5 cm) and 24½" (62.3 cm) laths, to identify them as vertical laths. Using colored pen, mark the letter S on the 10" (25.5 cm) and 3¼" (8.2 cm) spacers. Using a pencil, mark right side of all remaining laths with an H, for horizontal laths.

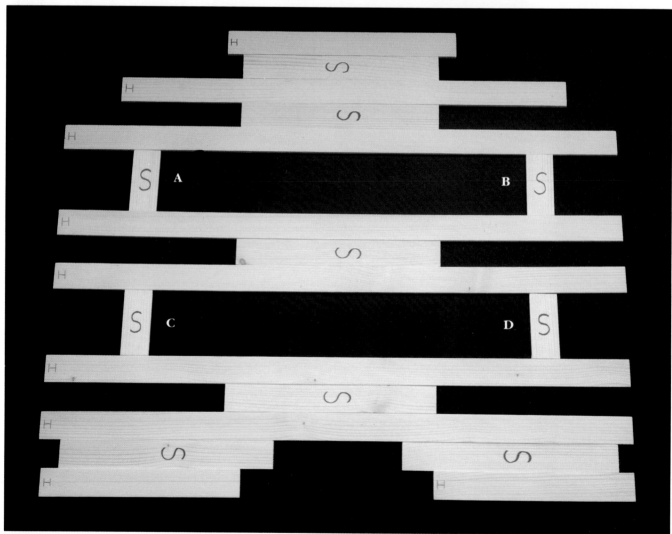

2 Lay out horizontal laths, right sides up, as shown. Place the spacers between laths, to separate them evenly; use 3¼" (8.2 cm) spacers vertically as indicated at A, B, C, and D. Check for symmetrical placement of laths.

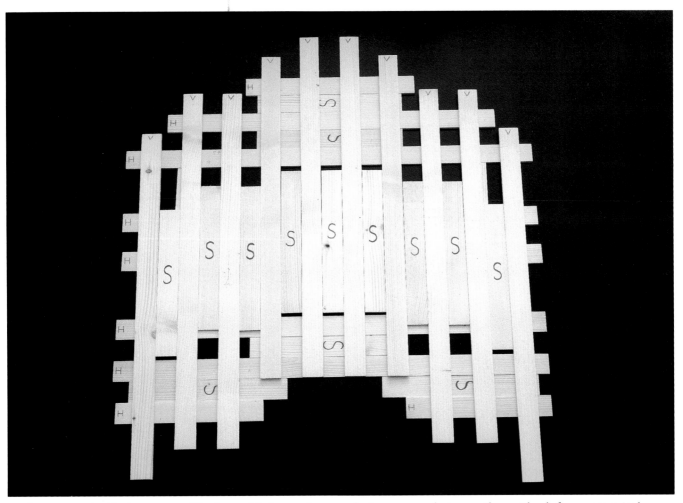

3 Lay out vertical laths on top of horizontal laths, as shown, placing spacers between them. Check for symmetrical placement of laths.

4 Lift the vertical laths, and apply glue sparingly to the top side of horizontal laths at all overlapping areas of lattice, spreading glue with finger; lift and secure one vertical lath at a time, working from one side of lattice to the other. Do not apply glue to spacers.

5 Allow glue to set for 15 minutes. Weight lattice strips down; allow to dry overnight to ensure a secure bond.

(Continued)

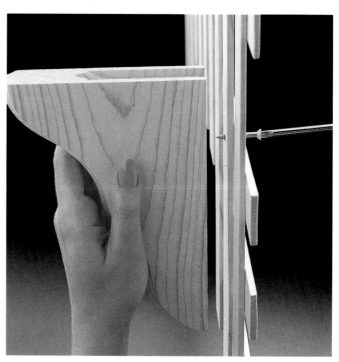

6 Remove spacers; turn lattice over to wrong side. For placement of screws, measure 8" (20.5 cm) from the bottom of the second vertical lath on each side; mark the middle of the intersection of horizontal and vertical laths. Centerpunch with awl; using 1/8" drill bit, predrill holes at marks, drilling through horizontal and vertical laths.

7 Mark placement for screw on the back edge of each bracket, measuring 2" (5 cm) down from the top of the bracket. Centerpunch brackets with awl; predrill holes, using 1/8" drill bit. Align brackets to lattice at predrilled holes; attach, using 8 × 1 1/4" (3.2 cm) wood screws.

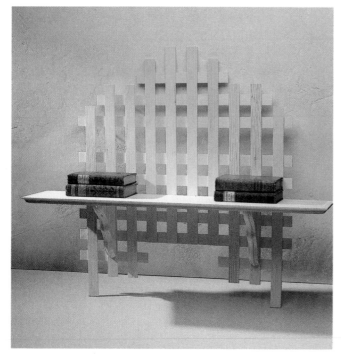

8 Miter and secure molding to sides and front of shelf as on page 110, steps 1 to 3; in step 3, secure moldings flush with top edge of shelf. Secure shelf to top side of brackets, using wood glue and centering shelf. Lean the shelf at an angle; weight down for 3 or 4 hours, until glue has dried.

9 Apply aerosol paint to lattice shelf; allow to dry. Mark screw placement for swivel hangers directly above the bracket screws at middle of shelf. Centerpunch with awl; predrill holes, using 1/8" drill bit. Attach swivel hangers, using 6 × 1" (2.5 cm) brass screws.

MORE IDEAS FOR LATTICE SHELVES

Lattice with multiple shelves *is constructed following the same basic method as on pages 119 to 122. The laths are cut so the completed latticework measures 16" × 50" (40.5 × 127 cm). A single-shelf variation in this width is shown on page 6.*

Stained moldings *(right), called window stop, are used instead of laths for this 5" × 48" (12.5 × 122 cm) multiple shelf.*

COLLECTIONS

Collections add character and charm to a kitchen and are a reflection of your interests. Showcase your grandmother's Depression glass on a plate rail. Hang baskets from the ceiling with bundles of dried flowers and herbs. Nestle pottery above the cabinets. Or tuck your country finds into an open jelly cabinet.

If you have not already started a collection, the process of finding interesting pieces can be as enjoyable as showing them off. Flea markets, antique sales, estate auctions, and resale shops are bursting at the seams with a wide variety of collectibles. When shopping, consider the condition or quality of the item. While hat boxes, wooden milk crates, and folk art are sometimes more charming in a worn state, you may prefer to shop for dinnerware items that are in good condition.

Collections need not be limited to display use. Many can also serve as everyday or special-occasion pieces. Serve mint jelly from an antique canning jar and pour milk from a country milk bottle. Or arrange a small grouping of collectibles for a table centerpiece.

Cookie jars *create a whimsical display.*

Copper antiques *(opposite) add warmth and charm to a kitchen.*

Advertising art *is grouped as a wallscape in this country kitchen. On the small shelf, old tea and coffee tins are used as plant holders.*

Corked bottles *are filled with herbal oils and vinegars for a colorful display.*

INDEX

CREDITS

CY DECOSSE INCORPORATED

A COWLES MAGAZINES COMPANY

Chairman/CEO: Bruce Barnet
Chairman Emeritus: Cy DeCosse
President/COO: Nino Tarantino
Executive V.P./Editor-in-Chief:
William B. Jones

DECORATING THE KITCHEN
Created by: The Editors of
Cy DeCosse Incorporated

Also available from the publisher:
*Bedroom Decorating, Creative Window
Treatments, Decorating for Christmas,
Decorating the Living Room, Creative
Accessories for the Home, Decorating
with Silk & Dried Flowers, Kitchen &
Bathroom Ideas, Decorative Painting,
Decorating Your Home for Christmas,
Decorating for Dining & Entertaining,
Decorating with Fabric & Wallcovering,
Decorating the Bathroom, Decorating
with Great Finds*

Group Executive Editor: Zoe A. Graul
Senior Technical Director: Rita C. Arndt
Senior Project Manager: Joseph Cella
Project Manager: Diane Dreon
Senior Art Director: Lisa Rosenthal
Art Director: Stephanie Michaud
Writer: Rita C. Arndt
Editor: Janice Cauley
Researcher/Designer: Michael Basler
Research Assistant: Linda Neubauer
Sample Supervisor: Carol Olson
Senior Technical Photo Stylist: Bridget
Haugh
Technical Photo Stylist: Susan Pasqual
Styling Director: Bobbette Destiche
Crafts Stylists: Coralie Sathre, Joanne
Wawra
Assistant Crafts Stylist: Deanna Despard
Artisans: Sharon Ecklund, Corliss
Forstrom, Phyllis Galbraith, Linda
Neubauer, Carol Pilot, Nancy Sundeen
*Vice President of Development Planning
& Production:* Jim Bindas
Director of Photography: Mike Parker
Creative Photo Coordinator: Cathleen
Shannon
Assistant Studio Manager: Marcia
Chambers
Lead Photographer: Mike Parker
Photographers: Stuart Block, Rebecca
Hawthorne, Mike Hehner, Rex Irmen,
Bill Lindner, Mark Macemon, Paul
Najlis, Charles Nields, Robert Powers

Contributing Photographers: Howard
Kaplan, Paul Markert, Brad Parker
Production Manager: Amelia Merz
Senior Desktop Publishing Specialist: Joe
Fahey
Production Staff: Adam Esco, Mike
Hehner, Jeff Hickman, Janet Morgan,
Robert Powers, Mike Schauer, Kay
Wethern, Nik Wogstad
Shop Supervisor: Phil Juntti
Scenic Carpenters: John Nadeau, Mike
Peterson, Greg Wallace
Consultants: Raymond W. Arndt, Sr.,
Amy Engman, Wendie Fedie, Gretchen
Graul, Patrick Kartes, Michael Lane,
Sharon Lock, Nadine Millot, Susan
Palmquest, La Rue Despard Shore,
Susan Wiley
Contributors: American Art Clay Co., Inc.;
American Standard; Armstrong Flooring;
Chicken Chairs; Crystal Kitchens;
Designs by "Brentwood"; Duncan
Enterprises; Formica Corp.; Waverly,
Division of F. Schumacher & Company
Printed on American paper by:
R. R. Donnelley & Sons (0795)

Cy DeCosse Incorporated offers
a variety of how-to books. For
information write:
Cy DeCosse Subscriber Books
5900 Green Oak Drive
Minnetonka, MN 55343